DREAMS & TRADITIONS

300 Years of British and Irish Painting from the collection of the Ulster Museum

Eileen Black
S. B. Kennedy
W. A. Maguire

Published by
The Ulster Museum, Belfast
in association with the Smithsonian Instituition
Traveling Exhibition Service

1997

ULSTER MUSEUM
Botanic Gardens Belfast BT9 5AE

Published on the occasion of an exhibition
organized by the Smithsonian Instituition
Traveling Exhibition Service (SITES)
and the Ulster Museum

ISBN 0 9000761 32 6

Dreams and Traditions: 300 Years of British
and Irish Painting from the
Collection of the Ulster Museum

Ulster Museum Publication No. 274

British Library Cataloguing in Publication Data. A catalogue
record for this book is available from the British Library.

COVER
Thomas Bate (worked c. 1690),
*Thomas, Lord Coningsby (1656-1729),
seated in a romanticised landscape, with
a view of the North Prospect of Hampton Court,
Herefordshire in the background* (no. 2).

BACK
Basil Blackshaw (b. 1932), *The Barn (Blue II)* (no. 45).

Printed in Northern Ireland by W. & G. Baird Ltd.

Contents

Foreword

Dreams and Traditions is the second exhibition which the Ulster Museum has organised in collaboration with the Smithsonian Institution Traveling Exhibition Service. The first, *Portraits and Prospects*, took place in 1989 and featured a selection of British and Irish watercolours and drawings from the Museum's extensive holdings in that area. With *Dreams and Traditions*, the artist's vision is explored on a larger scale, through the medium of oil paint. The selection exhibited in this instance, British and Irish paintings from the second half of the seventeenth century to the present day, embraces a wide variety of styles and artistic outlook. On a personal note, I am delighted that this collection of works (a number of which are old favourites with the museum's regular public) is about to be seen by a wider audience, far beyond these shores.

Numerous members of staff have been involved in the exhibition, namely Dr Jim McGreevy, Joanne Quayle and Lyn Stinson of the Conservation Department, Gerry Watters, who designed the catalogue, Pat McLean and Sandra Neill in the Marketing and Development Department and Sylvia Frawley, Registrar; my thanks to them. Particular thanks to the authors of the essays - Eileen Black, Dr S. B. Kennedy and Dr W. A. Maguire - whose lively and informative texts have helped illuminate and clarify the paintings and the period. A special vote of gratitude to Eileen Black, project leader of the exhibition, who also edited the catalogue and over the course of many months brought the project to completion.

A venture of this magnitude would not have been possible without the considerable financial assistance of The British Council, in association with the Department of Education for Northern Ireland; sincere thanks to Peter Lyner, Director of the former and to Lynda Wilson, Assistant Director, for much practical help and support. Also, to those at SITES, namely Donald McClelland, former Assistant Director for Programs, Jeff Thompson, project director of *Dreams and Traditions* and their ancillary staff - I am grateful for much sterling work on their side of the Atlantic. Finally, thanks to the American sponsors of this catalogue, Paul Mellon and the H. J. Heinz Company Foundation, for their generous financial support towards this publication.

Marshall McKee
Acting Director
Ulster Museum

Acknowledgements

We at SITES are pleased to be able to bring to the United States the exhibition *Dreams and Traditions: 300 Years of British and Irish Painting from the Collection of the Ulster Museum*. This exhibition will allow audiences to experience a wide spectrum of paintings by eminent British and Irish artists collected by the Ulster Museum over the years.

The exhibition has been selected and organized by Donald McClelland, former Assistant Director for Programs at SITES, by Dr S.B. Kennedy, Head of Fine and Applied Art at the Ulster Museum and by Eileen Black, Curator of Fine Art. We thank them and their colleague Dr W.A. Maguire, Head of Human History and Acting Deputy Director, for their contributions to the exhibition and its catalogue. In the same institution, both Sandra Neill, Head of Marketing and Development and Sylvia Frawley, Registrar, worked to ensure the success of the exhibition's tour and catalogue. For their continued interest in the project we are also grateful to Marshall McKee, Acting Director of the Ulster Museum, to John C. Nolan, former Director and to Mervyn Solomon, a Trustee.

Major international exhibitions such as this can only succeed with the support of a variety of individuals and institutions. We are pleased that this is our second collaboration with both the Ulster Museum and The British Council. At The British Council, Northern Ireland, we would like to thank Peter Lyner, Director and Lynda Wilson, Assistant Director. At The British Council, U.S.A., we extend special gratitude to David Evans, Director; Carmel McGill, Northern Ireland Cultural Exchanges Officer and Susan Ainsley, Cultural Affairs Officer. The exhibition would not have been possible without the support of Peter Holmes, Under Secretary of the Department of Education for Northern Ireland. For funding in support of the catalogue we are grateful to Paul Mellon and the H.J. Heinz Company Foundation.

At SITES we thank Jeff Thompson, Project Director and Mary Sipper, former Project Director; also Andrea Stevens, Associate Director for External Relations and Fredric Williams, Assistant Director for Programs. For designing and producing the exhibition's panels and labels, we thank, from the Smithsonian Institution's Office of Exhibits Central: Michael Headley, Director; Mary Bird, Supervisor, Design, Editing and Graphics; Eve MacIntyre, Visual Specialist and Rosemary Regan, Editor. As the exhibition begins its tour in the spring of 1997, we extend our gratitude to the institutions hosting *Dreams and Traditions* for their energetic role in acquainting their audiences with the extraordinarily rich variety of British and Irish paintings in the Ulster Museum.

Anna R. Cohn

Director, Smithsonian Institution Traveling Exhibition Service (SITES)

Introduction

The diversity of genres and styles characteristic of British and Irish painting over the last three centuries is reflected in this selection of works from the Ulster Museum, Northern Ireland's premier painting collection. Taken together, the paintings tell the complex story of two countries, the beliefs and experiences of their peoples and the lands that witnessed their history and nurtured their dreams.

The Ulster Museum's collection of British and Irish paintings brings together a rich variety of works by a number of eminent artists. The many artistic connections between Britain and Ireland were brought about by the relative ease of travel between both countries over the centuries and London's emergence, in the eighteenth century, as a conduit for advances in European art. Thus Sir Joshua Reynolds, whose works were the height of sophistication in portraiture at the time, was called upon to paint an Irish sitter, Theodosia Magill (no. 8), replete with the antique-inspired background detail and ennobling pose characteristic of his finest portraits of British figures. Similarly, the Irish landscapist George Barret, so admirably represented here by a view of the waterfall at Powerscourt, County Wicklow (no. 10), was an early exponent of the Sublime in romantic landscape, who based many of his precepts on the philosophical writings of Edmund Burke and who also pursued a career in London for many years.

The interchange of artists and ideas between the two countries often yielded paintings which served one side or another in the many political upheavals over the centuries. The London artist Thomas Mitchell imaginatively embellished his view of the river Boyne (no. 6) with such elements as foliage, golden light and a fanciful statue of William III, probably reflecting the demands of the person who commissioned the painting. This bombastic view of the river avoids the deep significance which the Boyne has had for Irish culture over many centuries, as it ran through the historically rich County Meath and carried the name (derived from Boand) of one of the chief goddesses of pre-Christian Ireland.

Both Irish and British artists often looked outside the British Isles for inspiration and could end up with remarkably different results. Like the members of the Norwich School, with whom he exhibited, Joseph Paul (no. 23) looked to the Dutch School for guidance but used such lessons only to enhance the Englishness of his scene. Roderic O'Conor (no. 31), on the other hand, embraced the work of the Pont Aven painters in the circle of Gauguin, leading contributors to Post-Impressionism. O'Conor assimilated so many lessons from these painters so adeptly that it is only after long reflection over his brilliant canvases that one begins to discern glimpses of his native character.

The exhibition ends with an artist indigenous to Northern Ireland who remained there to transform his experiences of the land into painted expression, Basil Blackshaw (no. 45). Residing in the Lagan Valley, Blackshaw captured in his works the abiding vitality of the region.

All the artists in the exhibition reflect the various stages of the history of painting in Britain and Ireland. Many were brought into direct contact with famed sights, which inspire us today with their mellifluous names: Glendalough, Killarney, Ballycastle. The artists of these islands profoundly understood those natural and spiritual threads that helped weave the fabric of which a land and a people are made. The magnificent paintings in this exhibition will surely reach an appreciative audience in North America, one ready to listen to the echoes of these countries and their histories.

Donald R. McClelland

Painting in Britain and Ireland 1660-1900

The restoration of the British monarchy in 1660, after the Civil War and the Protectorate of Oliver Cromwell, brought not only a sustained period of peace to Ireland which lasted almost thirty years but also saw the beginning of a tradition of fine and decorative art in a country which had been wracked by strife and successive waves of English colonisation since 1534. There are few extant paintings known to have been executed in Ireland before the seventeenth century and evidence of artistic tradition prior to that time is confined mainly to tomb monuments and frescoes at religious sites such as Holy Cross and Cashel.[1] That painters were working in the country in the early years of the seventeenth century is known from the diaries of the Earl of Cork, who in 1621 commissioned a French artist to paint a collection of family portraits for him. Most portraits from this period and earlier are of the Anglo-Irish upper class and English settler class, like that of Captain William Jackson, which opens this selection of paintings. Portraits of the native Irish, on the other hand, are extremely scarce.

Whereas seventeenth century England saw the architectural splendours of Inigo Jones, Sir Christopher Wren and others, Ireland lacked sophisticated architecture on a grand scale. The great Irish houses of the seventeenth century were robust fortified dwellings, with few examples of fine and decorative art. However, under the first viceroy of the Restoration period, James Butler, Duke of Ormonde, the situation changed. A devotee and patron of the arts, Ormonde decorated his residence, Kilkenny Castle, with wall and ceiling paintings, easel paintings and tapestries and installed a gallery, which (according to a visitor in 1698), '... for length, variety of gilded chairs, and the curious pictures that adorn it, has no equal in the three kingdoms [that is, England, Scotland and Ireland], and perhaps not in Europe.'[2]

Ormonde's viceroyalty, which lasted from 1661 to 1669, ushered in a period of prosperity in Dublin. Between 1660 and 1685, the population of the capital doubled, extensive building schemes were carried out and the city became a mecca for merchants, craftsmen and artists.[3] During this time, the first society for the arts in Ireland, namely the Cutlers, Painter Stainers and Stationery Company of Dublin (known as the Guild of St Luke the Evangelist) was established in 1670.[4] Amongst its members were Thomas Pooley (1646-1723), who painted many of the Anglo-Irish in the 1680s and Garret Morphey (d. 1716), the first Irish-born artist of consequence. Morphey, who combined English and Continental influences in his portraiture and raised the quality of Irish art from its early provincialism, included Williamites and Jacobites amongst his patrons.

Amongst non-Irish artists drawn to Dublin during this period were Gaspar Smitz from Holland (d. c. 1707), the Scot John Michael Wright (1617-94) and Thomas Bate, a tantalisingly obscure figure who is best known for his portrait of Thomas, Lord Coningsby (no. 2), a leading Williamite, painted in 1692. Smitz, like Bate a portrait painter, worked also as a picture restorer and has left a vivid account of his employment in this line, in a letter of January 1685 to his patron, Sir John Perceval. In addition to providing fascinating information on a seventeenth century restorer at work, the letter, quoted at length in *The Painters of Ireland*, indicates that there were many paintings in Ireland by the 1680s.[5]

The most illustrious of these late seventeenth century visitors to Dublin was the above-mentioned John Michael Wright, active in the city 1679-80. Amongst his several commissions was a portrait of the Jacobite Sir Neil O'Neill of Killelagh dressed as an Irish chieftain, painted in 1680 (versions of which are in Dunrobin Castle, Sutherland and the Tate Gallery). This work, one of the most remarkable to be produced in the country, is an evocative and haunting image of Gaelic Ireland, by that stage almost decimated by English colonisation. (The only other known depiction of early Irish dress is Marcus Gheeraert's portrait of Captain Thomas Lee of 1594, likewise Tate Gallery, which shows Lee bare-legged like an Irish foot-soldier and wearing dress derived from a costume book). O'Neill's adoption of Irish dress was both a nostalgic longing for a vanished age and an emotional commitment to an Irish ideal, which for him culminated in his fight for the Jacobite cause at the Battle of the Boyne in 1690.

The first half of the eighteenth century in Ireland brought a growing sophistication in portraiture and the development of landscape painting. Portrait painting during this period was dominated by a single figure, that of James Latham (1696-1747). Irish by birth, Latham studied abroad and subsumed into his style the blend of realism and formality common in French portraiture of the period. This elegance and ease of manner can be seen in his portrait of Captain de la Bouchetière (no. 3), painted 1730-35. Amongst Latham's contemporaries, though of lesser stature, were Charles Jervas (c. 1675-1739), an absentee Irish painter who returned home on a regular basis and the English artists John Lewis (fl. 1740-69) and Stephen Slaughter (1697-1765), both of whom established careers in Ireland. Lewis, best known as a theatrical scene painter, was also a gifted portraitist, as shown by his sensitive study of an unknown man (no. 5), painted in 1748.

With landscape painting, progress was slower in Ireland than in England. In the latter country in the 1690s, the Dutch artist Jan Wyck (c. 1640-1702) used broad panoramas as background for his numerous Battle of the Boyne scenes and influenced later painters such as John Wootton (d. 1756) and the latter's pupil George Lambert (1700-65), both of whom were executing landscapes in the manner of Gaspard Poussin by the 1720s and 1730s.[6] Professional topographers like Leonard Knyff (1650-1721) were also producing bird's-eye views of gentlemen's parks in England from the late seventeenth century. In Ireland, on the other hand, the first important figure in landscape painting - William van der Hagen (d. 1745) - did not emerge until the 1720s. Hitherto, the depiction of landscape in Ireland had been the preserve of engravers, map makers and travellers such as the antiquarian Francis Place (1647-1728). Van der Hagen's output was varied and included imaginary views, classical landscapes and port scenes. In his last known work, a picturesque view of Powerscourt waterfall, engraved in 1745, he moved from formal topography into the realms of romantic landscape.

With this blossoming of fine art in Ireland in the first half of the eighteenth century came the establishment of the first art educational institution in the country, namely Robert West's drawing school, supported by the Dublin Society from 1746 and taken over by it in 1750.[7] The Dublin Society had been founded in 1731 by members of the ruling Anglo-Irish ascendancy, with the aim of 'improving Husbandry, Manufactures and other Useful Arts.'[8] Its arts committee was set up shortly thereafter. From 1746, prizes (premiums) for West's best students - and the Society's best students from 1750 - were awarded by the Society's first benefactor, Dr Samuel Madden. The Society's schools, which embraced figure drawing, landscape and ornament and architectural drawing, became the major focus of art instruction in Ireland over the next hundred years and through the French bias of the teaching staff, helped raise an awareness of Continental art amongst would-be Irish artists.[9] A school of modelling was added in 1811.

Besides art instruction for students (which was free), the Society also gave prizes for the encouragement of the fine arts through public competition (likewise financed by Madden). Madden urged the gentry to give thought to the decoration of their homes and was keen to advance 'those politer arts, which are in a manner strangers to our country; I mean Sculpture, Painting and Architecture ... We should at least aim so far to employ and enrich our People by them, as may both spur on their Industry, improve our Taste, and adorn our Country.'[10] The awarding of prizes to encourage the arts was already current in France and Italy. Madden's scheme came into operation in 1740, when the first prize was given to the artist Susanna Drury (fl. 1733-70), for four landscapes of the Giant's Causeway, Country Antrim (two of which are in the Ulster Museum), painted c. 1739. The Society's prizes, altered from cash payments to medals in 1767, continued to be awarded for many years. A similar scheme, on Dublin Society lines, was adopted by the Society of Arts in London in 1754.

The second half of the eighteenth century saw sufficient patronage in Ireland to support several portrait and landscape painters and a number of artists pursued successful careers in Dublin (and in Belfast, to a much lesser extent). These years also saw the establishment of the first exhibiting society in the country in 1765 - the Society of Artists in Ireland - which held regular exhibitions until 1780 and which was modelled on the Society of Artists in London.[11] Its creation was an indication of rising public interest in the arts. Amongst portraitists, Robert Hunter (1715/20 - c. 1803) reigned supreme in Dublin from the 1750s to the 1780s and had a varied clientele which included professional persons and landed families.[12] An artist with much more flair than the somewhat pedestrian Hunter was Hugh Douglas Hamilton (1740-1808), well known in Dublin as a pastellist by the 1760s. On returning to Ireland in 1792, after years spent in London and Italy, he achieved great success as a painter in oils. During this second flowering of his career in Ireland, he portrayed numerous members of fashionable society and patriots such as John Philpot Curran, Lord Edward Fitzgerald (a version of which is in the Ulster Museum) and James Moore O'Donnell (no. 14), painted c. 1795-6.

Visiting portrait painters also made their mark on Dublin during this time, perhaps none more so than the English artist Francis Wheatley (1747-1801), resident in the captial 1779-83.[13] His paintings of Volunteer meetings and of the Irish House of Commons during Grattan's parliament, images of patriotism and of the struggle for legislative independence from England, have acquired an heroic significance for Irish people down the centuries. His portrait of Viscount O'Neill of c. 1780, a member of the above parliament, is included here as number 17. The work may perhaps be related to another portrait of O'Neill in the large Irish House of Commons painting of 1780, referred to above (Leeds City Art Galleries). Other visiting artists included Robert Home (1752-1834), a native of Hull, in Dublin 1779-89 and the American, Gilbert Stuart (1755-1828), whose stay extended from 1787 to 1793. Home's patrons included academics at Trinity College, Dublin, whilst Stuart's were mainly connected with the Irish House of Commons.

Inevitably, in this period as in others, a number of Irish artists chose to pursue their careers elsewhere. The best known were Nathaniel Hone (1718-84) and James Barry (1741-

1806). Hone settled in London as a young man and only returned to Ireland occasionally. Renowned as a portrait painter, his particular forte was children, of whom he had ten, whom he frequently depicted in attractive works such as *A Boy deliberating on his Drawing*, c. 1766 (no. 7) and *The Piping Boy*, 1769 (National Gallery of Ireland). Barry, the opposite of Hone in subject matter, specialized in history and mythological and biblical scenes on the grand scale. A driven, aggressive figure whose chief interest was in the antique and in classical art, he studied in France and Italy 1765-70 and thereafter became the foremost neo-classical painter in England. Other less renowned emigrants included Thomas Hickey (fl. 1756-1816), who spent much of his working life in India and Matthew William Peters (1742-1814), who, before he became an Anglican priest in 1783, had a reputation as a painter of nubile young women of questionable character.

Landscape painting made considerable progress during the second half of the eighteenth century in centres such as Cork and Waterford as well as Dublin. Concurrent with this development was a preference by Irish collectors for Dutch cabinet pictures. This fondness of the Irish gentry for Dutch and also Flemish art is reflected in Irish landscape painting although Italian influence can also be seen on occasion, as for example in *Landscape with Figures* (no. 4), by the Waterford artist Richard Carver (d. 1754). Here, the figures in contemporary dress are decidedly northern yet the overall appearance of the work is classical. Much more Italianate in flavour but by an English visitor to Ireland in the late 1750s - Thomas Mitchell (1735-90) - is *A view of the River Boyne with gentlemen and horses by a statue to William III in the foreground, the Boyne obelisk beyond*, 1757 (no. 6). In this painting, the Boyne valley is transmuted into an idealized Claudean landscape, bathed in mellow golden light.

Irish landscape painting reached its zenith during these years in the work of Thomas Roberts (1748-78) and William Ashford (1746-1824). Roberts, the most brilliant landscapist of the time, was sadly short-lived, dying at the age of thirty. His legacy is a series of picturesque views of parks of the nobility of Ireland, evocative and nostalgic images of a vanished age. Ashford likewise specialized in well-ordered estates and country seats, rendered with a distinctly English air. A native of Birmingham and the foremost painter in Ireland in the late eighteenth century, he rarely tackled the wild and romantic scenery favoured by most Irish landscapists of the time. Typical of his work is *Landscape with Carriage and Horses* (no. 11), a topographical view verging on the picturesque.

The best known of those who pursued romantic landscape painting in Ireland was George Barret (1728/32-84), Ashford's near-contemporary. Well established as an artist before 1763, when he moved to London, he regularly painted in the scenic Powerscourt estate in County Wicklow in his early career. *The Waterfall at Powerscourt* (no. 10) dates from this time. Regarded until recently as a somewhat poor follower of Richard Wilson (1713?-82) (who described Barret's foliage scathingly as 'spinach and eggs'), he is now recognised as being amongst the forerunners of romantic landscape painting.[14] Of other landscapists to the fore at this time, probably none made a greater impact than Jonathan Fisher (d. 1809), who helped popularize Irish scenery through his engravings and acquatints of various parts of Ireland, published by himself from his own originals. Though somewhat stiff at times and lacking in atmosphere, his paintings - of which *View of the Ferry and Castle of Narrow Water*, c. 1771 (no. 9) is a typical example - are appealing and valuable images of place.

Mention has been made of Belfast. A small and commercially-focused town, more Scottish and Presbyterian in character than Irish, Belfast at this time was an artistic back-water compared with Dublin, the political and cultural capital of Ireland. Nevertheless, the town supported three artists, two of them simultaneously - Strickland Lowry (1737-c. 85), Joseph Wilson (fl. c. 1766-93) and Thomas Robinson (d. 1810) - and was visited by a number of others, 'straggling adventurers of the brush,' who were merely passing through on the road to greater advancement elsewhere.[15] Picture buying in Belfast at this period was largely directed towards portraiture and Lowry, Wilson and Robinson concentrated their energies on this. Lowry, the first artist of repute to work in the town, was at the height of his powers in the 1760s, when he painted two large group portraits of two of Belfast's leading merchant families, the Batesons (Ulster Museum) and the Gregs (private collection).[16] However, by 1780 and nearing the end of his career, his abilities declined and his figures became somewhat wooden in appearance, as evidenced by *Portrait of a Lady* (no. 12), painted in that year. Nevertheless, despite their almost primitive appearance, his late works, of which this is a fine example, have considerable charm.

Joseph Wilson, Lowry's main rival for business, was well established by the mid-1760s and flourished until the 1780s. His patrons were generally from the professional and merchant classes such as Hugh Hyndman (no. 13), painted about 1782 in Volunteer uniform. Probably in response to demand, Wilson also executed portraits on small oval-shaped wooden panels, which he presumably sold at low cost. His works, whilst uneven in standard, are valuable records of late eighteenth century Ulster society. Robinson, the third leading artist, had a varied clientele which included business men like William Ritchie (no. 18), painted about 1802 and nobility such as the Earl of Massereene. Active about ten years after Lowry and Wilson, he experienced considerable financial hardship in Belfast during the late 1790s. Events surrounding his career reinforce the impression that the town at this time was ruled by commerce above all else. Perhaps in the hope of an improvement in circumstances, he moved to Dublin towards the end of his life.

The improved condition of the fine arts in Ireland in the second half of the eighteenth century, shown by a growth in patronage and a rising awareness of art through exhibitions, was mirrored - on a larger scale - by artistic events in England at the same time. There, the Society of Artists was established in 1760 and held regular exhibitions in London until 1791.[17] In 1761, seceders from this group formed the Free Society of Artists, organised on charitable lines for the relief of financially distressed artists and their dependents. This society held exhibitions until 1783. Both bodies became useful platforms for the fine arts. Of greater import, however, was the founding of the Royal Academy in 1768, an institution which owed its early sucess to the patronage of George III and to the drive and ambition of its first president, Sir Joshua Reynolds (1723-92).[18]

The advent of Reynolds was a turning point in British painting.[19] Erudite and intellectual (at a time when most British artists were poorly- educated tradesmen), Reynolds made allusion to the Old Masters and to antique sculpture the basis of his art. In consequence, by his absorption of the Italian Grand Style and his use of it in a British context, he helped raise both the status of the artist in British society and of portraiture as a genre. The painting of Theodosia Magill of c. 1765 (no.8) is typical of his style; the sitter is shown not in contemporary dress but in the loose 'nightgown' which Reynolds insisted upon, as being more classical in appearance and less subject to the whims of fashion. A further reference to the classical is displayed by the inclusion of a large antique vase, the design of which is derived from the sixteenth century Italian artist, Polidoro da Caravaggio. Almost every person of consequence in British society in the second half of the eighteenth century sat to Reynolds.

Between the age of Reynolds and the age of Sir Thomas Lawrence (1769-1830), whose glittering portraits seem to encapsulate the splendours of the Regency period of the early nineteenth century, portraiture in Britain was dominated by George Romney (1734-1802). Amongst portraitists of lesser standing were John Hoppner (1758-1810), Sir William Beechey (1753-1839) and Sir Henry Raeburn (1756-1823), the latter the leading painter in the 'Athens of the North', namely Edinburgh. Of the three, Beechey was renowned for his straightforward and truthful likenesses, with little of the showiness of Hoppner and Raeburn. This sobriety of approach can be seen clearly in his sensitive and dignified portrait of an elderly woman, painted about 1785-95 (no.16).

Of the numerous British artists of the second half of the eighteenth century, however, few have left such memorable images as Joseph Wright of Derby (1734-97), the first professional painter to make scenes of the Industrial Revolution his subject matter.[20] A friend and associate of scientists and industrialists in Derby through his membership of the Lunar Society, Wright's well-known scientific scenes by candlelight date from the 1760s. Of these, *An Experiment on a Bird in the Air Pump*, 1768 (Tate Gallery) is his masterpiece. His chief interest, however, was in the effect of light, a motif which dominates much of his output. A trip to Italy in 1773-5, during which he saw Vesuvius erupting, awakened him to the possibilities of combining his interest in light with landscape painting. Thereafter he painted Derbyshire views under unusual conditions of sunlight or moonlight. *Virgil's Tomb: Sun Breaking through a Cloud*, 1785 (no.15), with its characteristic focus on light, was painted in England from sketches made in Italy.

In 1800 Ireland united with England under the Act of Union, the beginning of the century was, metaphorically, a new beginning for Ireland. With the abolition of the Irish parliment, the character of Dublin society changed, as many nobility and gentry either moved to London or settled in the country; before 1800, 300 members of parliment had Dublin residences, whereas by 1821, only five had houses in the city.[21] In this now somewhat homogenized society, patronage declined, as the new middle classes were not generally picture buyers. The early decades of the century, however, saw numerous art exhibitions by several art societies which set up and then folded. The premier art society, the Royal Hibernian Academy, was established in 1823, modelled on the Royal Academy in London. It continues to this day, an important feature of the Irish art world.

Of the several portrait painters in Dublin in the first half of the nineteenth century, Martin Cregan (1788-1870), first secretary of the above-mentioned Royal Hibernian Academy and its president 1832-57, was the leading exponent. Highly prolific, he exhibited 334 pictures at the Academy 1826-59. His portrait of Francis Johnston and family (no.22), painted c. 1827, is a fine example of his work. Johnston, an architect, likewise had connections with the Academy, being a founder member and builder, at his own expense, of the Academy's first premises in Abbey Street, Dublin, an important piece of patronage. Other portraitists of the period included William Cuming (1769-1852), Martin Archer Shee (1769-1850) and Adam Buck (1759-1833), who specialized in miniatures.

Landscape painting was pursued by a wide cross-section of artists in Ireland during these years, from painters of the first rank such as James Arthur O'Connor (1792-1841) to amateurs like the Belfast surgeon and watercolourist James Moore (1819-83). *The Patron, or the Festival of St Kevin at the Seven Churches, Glendalough*, 1813 (no.19) by Joseph Peacock (c. 1783-1837), an artist best known for his scenes of country fairs, features an expressive and dominant background landscape in what is essentially a genre painting.[22] Peacock has exaggerated the height of the round tower and mountains, to add drama to the terrain and make the scene more picturesque. Though he described himself as a 'Familiar Life and Animal Painter', he was obviously gifted at landscape. Interesting genre details also feature in *The Eagle's Nest, Killarney* (no.20), a landscape by Peacock's close contemporary, William Sadler II (c. 1782-1839). One of three generations of artists of the same name, Sadler II also painted Irish topical and historical subjects. The painting, which appropriately shows tourists at a well-known beauty spot in the Lakes, is of a higher quality than many of Sadler's other works, which tend to be uneven in standard.

The most able landscapists of the period, however, were George Petrie (1790-1866), James Arthur O'Connor and Francis Danby (1793-1861). Petrie, who remained in Dublin and worked only in watercolour, was also an author and antiquarian of repute, whilst Danby, who spent much of his career outside Ireland, achieved acclaim with large apocalyptic works in the manner of John Martin (1789-1854). Like Danby, O'Connor chose to settle elsewhere but continued to paint Irish scenery from memory. His work passed through various styles, from the purely topographical, through the picturesque, to the brooding romanticism of his later period from about 1830. *Scene in County Wicklow*, 1820 (no.21) dates from his picturesque phase.

The artistic lives of the above-mentioned portraitists and landscapists centred generally upon Dublin at various points of their careers. Belfast likewise produced and supported a number of artists at this period, albeit considerably fewer than the capital. Amongst painters in the north, Samuel Hawksett (1801-59) and Richard Hooke (1820-1908) reigned supreme as portraitists, as did Hugh Frazer (1813-61), James Howard Burgess (1817-90) and Andrew Nicholl (1804-86) with landscape. A lesser-known practitioner of the latter genre was James Glen Wilson (1827-63), who was working around Belfast in the early 1850s. His depiction of an *Emigrant Ship leaving Belfast*, 1852 (no. 24), probably en route to America, is a moving image of the sadness of emigration and is one of few known paintings relating to the subject.

A trend within Irish painting from the 1830s was a focus on Celtic-related subject matter, such as ancient ruins, high crosses and events from Irish mythology and folk life.[23] Antiquarians like George Petrie (above) were to the fore in this 'Celtic Revival', as it is called. Interest in national identity, of an awareness of cultural differences from England, accelerated from the passing of Catholic Emancipation in 1829; this curiosity about Irishness, initially confined to middle-class scholars and antiquarians, eventually spread throughout the entire country. Emblems such as the round tower, harp and shamrock became powerful expressions of Irishness. The view of ancient ruins at Holy Island, Lough Derg of c. 1863 (no. 25), by Bartholomew Colles Watkins (1833-91), a romanticised and dramatic image of early Christian Ireland, is a product of this swell of national feeling. Of greater impact than the visual arts in this expression of nationalism, however, was the written word. Over the years, Irish identity grew increasingly bound up with the language and culture of the early Irish, a rich source of material which was mined by numerous authors and poets. More than anyone else, the poet and dramatist William Butler Yeats epitomises this Celtic Revival in literature - the movement known as the Irish Literary Renaissance - of the end of the century. His youthful portrait, included here as number 26, was painted in the same year - 1889 - in which he met his Muse, Maud Gonne, the inspiration for some of his finest poetry.

Unlike Irish painting of the nineteenth century, which produced few major figures (Francis Danby and Daniel Maclise (1808-70) being probably the best known), British painting of the period is filled with famous names: John Constable (1776-1837), J. M. W. Turner (1775-1851), Sir Edwin Landseer (1802-73) and many more. Queen Victoria's long reign, from 1837 until 1901, was an age of enormous artistic production; rich patrons such as James Leathart, John Miller, Robert Sheepshanks and Robert Vernon built up large collections of contemporary art whilst many artists not only amassed sizeable fortunes but also received knighthoods and baronetcies.[24] The sheer variety of Victorian painting is perhaps its most immediate characteristic. With animal and genre subjects, Landseer and William Powell Frith (1819-1909), in particular, created memorable images such as *The Monarch of the Glen*, 1851 (John Dewar and Sons Ltd.) and *The Derby Day*, 1856-8 (Tate Gallery), the latter a much-lauded example of the narrative realism made popular by Frith.

Amongst the most interesting (and nowadays amongst the best loved) of Victorian painters was the group known as the Pre-Raphaelite Brotherhood, established in 1848. Of its seven members, William Holman Hunt (1827-1910), John Everett Millais (1829-96) and Dante Gabriel Rossetti (1828-82) were the most important. Fellow artist Ford

Maddox Brown (1821-93), although not a member, was closely involved. Their work, which was generally serious in content and relied heavily on the use of symbols, was characterised by bright colour, naturalistic detail and intensity of feeling. Though they remained together as a group for only a short time, they left many memorable images, a number of which have since become virtual icons of the Victorian age, notably *Work*, 1852-65 by Brown (Manchester City Art Galleries), *The Scapegoat*, 1854 by Hunt (Lady Lever Art Gallery, Port Sunlight) and *The Awakening Conscience*, 1853-4 (Tate Gallery), likewise by Hunt. From the early 1860s, Rossetti and younger members of the circle, in particular Edward Coley Burne-Jones (1833-98), moved away from the vivid and hard-edged Pre-Raphaelite manner into the more poetic realms of the Aesthetic Movement. This, with its emphasis on beauty as an end in itself - art for art's sake - was also espoused by Frederic, Lord Leighton (1830-96), George Frederic Watts (1817-1904) and James McNeill Whistler (1834-1903) amongst others. Brooding beautiful women, sensual langour and voluptousness predominate in the work of the Movement's followers of the second half of the century

Landscape was produced in great quantity in Britain throughout the nineteenth century, by a multitude of worthy painters. Amongst the foremost in the tradition was John Constable, the first exemplar of naturalistic landscape, who painted the changing light of the English countryside - which he termed the 'chiaroscuro of nature' - in all its moods.[25] Probably the greatest exponent, however, was Turner, who explored the cosmic forces of nature in paintings in which smooth finish and detail counted for little and atmosphere and heightened emotion were paramount - as, for example, in *Slavers throwing overboard the Dead and Dying. Typhon coming on*, 1840 (Museum of Fine Arts, Boston). Others who also painted the Sublime in nature, in the manner of Turner, included John Martin and Francis Danby (the latter an expatriate Irishman). Their works in this genre have awe-inspiring titles such as *The Great Day of His Wrath*, 1851-3 (Martin, Tate Gallery) and *The Deluge*, 1837-40 (Danby, likewise Tate Gallery).

At a remove from this romantic interpretation of nature was the more prosaic approach of the Norwich School of landscape painters, whose models included seventeenth century Dutch landscape painting and Constable. Founded by John Crome (1768-1821) in 1803 as the Norwich Society of Artists, the painters of the School established a reputation for their picturesque views of the Norfolk countryside. *Mill Scene* (no. 23) by Joseph Paul of Norwich (1804-87), a follower of Crome, is derived from etchings by the latter. As is typical of the Norwich School, the picture is naturalistic in execution, with overtones of Dutch landscape painting.

In addition to these distinctive trends in landscape - the romantic and the Norwich School type - artists inevitably subsumed various other influences into their own particular styles. *Landscape with Windmill*, 1888 (no. 28), by Edmund Morison Wimperis (1835-1900), is atmospheric and expressive of the changing conditions of a windy day. Wimperis was influenced in this by Constable's near contemporary, David Cox (1783-1859), whose works are characterised by spontaneity and a freely handled style. These traits are also evident in *The Cherry Orchard* (no. 27) by John Clayton Adams (1840-1906), described by the Victorian art expert Christopher Wood as 'one of the most individual and least recognised of the late Victorian landscape painters.'[26] Evocative depictions of rural life, of haymakers toiling under the sun or children playing in an orchard, such as this, were popular subjects with landscapists of the late Victorian age.

During the second half of the nineteenth century and particularly from the 1870s, numerous British and Irish artists travelled abroad to complete their education, studying in Paris or Antwerp and spending their summers painting *en plein air* (that is, in the open air). This European study offered an alternative to the teaching methods of British and Irish art schools and was also a reaction to the academic subjects and the tight finish and artificial studio light of Academy-style paintings. The artists who followed this path, now known as the British and Irish Impressionists, espoused aims similar to those of the French Impressionists, namely an emphasis on light and the fleeting impression, captured in painting out of doors. (The term 'British Impressionists' and variants is useful but misleading, as the French Impressionists followed a particular scientific theory, whilst their British and other 'counterparts' did not. A more accurate description is '*plein air* painters'). In Britain, works by the French artists Millet, Corot, the Barbizon School, Manet and Degas had been shown in London in the 1870s by dealers such as Deschamps and Durand-Ruel. This helped spread knowledge of the French avant-garde.

Amongst the British Impressionists were John Singer Sargent (1856-1925), Whistler and Walter Sickert (1860-1942), of whom the latter two painted mainly urban subjects.[27] Also included were such as George Clausen (1852-1944), Stanhope Forbes (1857-1947) and Henry La Thangue (1859-1929), who were influenced by the square-brush technique and peasant subjects of the French *plein air* painter Jules Bastien-Lepage. In the background of these British painters of peasant themes was the dominating influence of Millet, the archetypal painter of peasant types. Forbes and a number of like-minded painters were instrumental in establishing a community of artists in the Cornish fishing village of Newlyn in the 1880s. Quaysides, village streets and fishing folk are typical Newlyn School subjects. Scottish painters were likewise involved in the exploration of Impressionism. Working mainly in and around Glasgow and concentrating largely on urban middle-class subjects, the 'Glasgow Boys', as they are called, included Joseph Crawhall (1861-1913), James Guthrie (1859-1930) and the Belfast-born John Lavery (1856-1941). (Examples of the latter's Impressionist works are in the Ulster Museum).

Of the Irish Impressionists, Nathaniel Hone (1831-1917) went to Paris as early as 1853 and spent almost twenty years in France, working in the village of Barbizon and in Brittany and Normandy.[28] His return to Ireland in 1872 may perhaps have influenced others to go in the later 1870s, such as Augustus Burke (c. 1849-91) and Aloysius O'Kelly (c. 1850/53 - c. 1926), both of whom were in Brittany about 1876. A number of others followed in the 1880s, including Nathaniel Hill (1861-1934), Joseph Malachy Kavanagh (1856-1918), Roderic O'Conor (1860-1940) and Walter Osborne (1859-1903). Frank O'Meara (1853-88), whose *Autumnal Sorrows*, 1878 is included here as number 29, settled at Grez-sur-Loing, a picturesque village in the forest of Fontainebleu, in 1875. A loner and seemingly depressive by nature, his paintings of peasant women at toil invariably exude feelings of sadness and melancholy. The best known Irish Impressionist, however, was Walter Osborne, who after working in Antwerp and Brittany, made Dublin his base from about 1884. His Impressionist subjects encompass rural scenes in England, figures in outdoor sunny settings as in the atmospheric portrait of J. B. S. MacIlwaine in his garden at Foxrock, painted in 1890 (National Gallery of Ireland) and street scenes around Dublin such as *Cherry Ripe*, 1889 (no. 30). Highly versatile as an artist, he was also the foremost portrait painter in Ireland by the end of the century.

As indicated in this brief outline, British and Irish painting of the period under review was a rich and varied tapestry, with many artistic cross-currents and links which space does not permit of discussion. Connections between the two islands were close, with London being the mecca for many Irish artists, before the exodus to Europe in the latter years of the nineteenth century. With the move to Impressionism, the avant-garde became a force to be reckoned with. Exciting new trends in art are the subject of the following essay.

Eileen Black
Curator of Fine Art

References

1. The basis of this essay is derived from Anne Crookshank and The Knight of Glin, *The Painters of Ireland c. 1660-1920* (London, 1978), a pioneering study in the history of fine art in Ireland.

2. Ibid., p. 16.

3. Jane Fenlon, 'The Painter Stainers Companies of Dublin and London, Craftsmen and Artists 1670-1740' in Jane Fenlon and Nicola Figgis (eds.), *New Perspectives: Studies in Art History in Honour of Anne Crookshank*, (Dublin, 1987), p. 101.

4. Ibid.

5. p. 21.

6. Ellis Waterhouse, *Painting in Britain 1530-1790* (Melbourne, London, Baltimore, 1953), p. 114. See also pp. 111-119.

7. See John Turpin, *A School of Art in Dublin since the Eighteenth Century* (Dublin, 1995) for a detailed account of art education in Dublin from the eighteenth century to the present day.

8. James Meenan and Desmond Clarke (eds.), *The Royal Dublin Society 1731-1981*, (Dublin, 1981), p. 1.

9. John Turpin, 'Continental influence in 18th century Ireland,' *Irish Arts Review*, vol. 4, no. 4, Winter 1987, p. 52.

10. Turpin, 1995, p. 10.

11. George Breeze, *Society of Artists in Ireland: Index of Exhibits, 1765-80* (Dublin, 1985).

12. See Anne Crookshank, 'Robert Hunter,' *Irish Arts Review*, Yearbook 1989-90, pp. 169-85.

13. Mary Webster, *Francis Wheatley* (London, 1970), pp. 29-52 contains a useful account of Wheatley's years in Ireland.

14. This remark by Wilson was related by William Beechey and recorded by Dawson Turner, in the latter's *Outlines in Lithography*, 1840, p. 91.

15. Quoted in *The Painters of Ireland*, p. 151.

16. The portrait of the Greg family is reproduced in John Cornforth, 'A Mill and its Master, *Country Life*, 28 December 1972, p. 1779.

17. See Algernon Graves, *The Society of Artists of Great Britain 1760-1791 and The Free Society of Artists 1761-1783* (Bath, 1969) for a useful history of both societies.

18. Sir Walter R. M. Lamb, *The Royal Academy: A Short History of its Foundation and Development* (London, 1951).

19. Waterhouse, 1953, contains useful chapters on Reynolds, fashionable portraiture and Wright of Derby.

20. For a fuller discussion on Wright, see Benedict Nicolson, *Joseph Wright of Derby* (London and New York, 1968) and Judy Egerton, *Wright of Derby*, exhibition catalogue, Tate Gallery, 1990.

21. *The Painters of Ireland*, p. 173.

22. The picture contains a wealth of information for the social historian. See W. H. Crawford, 'The Patron, or Festival of St. Kevin at the Seven Churches, Glendalough, County Wicklow 1813,' *Ulster Folklife*, vol. 32, 1986.

23. Jeanne Sheehy, *The Rediscovery of Ireland's Past: the Celtic Revival 1830-1930* (London, 1980) contains much useful information on this.

24. See Julian Treuherz, *Victorian Painting* (London, 1993) for an excellent introduction to the subject.

25. Jeremy Maas, *Victorian Painters* (London, 1970), p. 44.

26. Christopher Wood, *Victorian Painters* (Woodbridge, Suffolk, 1995), vol. 1, p. 18.

27. For information on the British Impressionists, see Kenneth McConkey, *British Impressionism* (Oxford, 1989).

28. Julian Campbell, *The Irish Impressionists: Irish Artists in France and Belgium, 1850-1914*, exhibition catalogue, National Gallery of Ireland, 1984.

British and Irish Painting in the Twentieth Century

Some years ago, writing about the development of British painting in the twentieth century the critic Richard Shone called his book *The Century of Change*,[1] for it was to change, notably in the form of the influences from European Modernism, that British painting had to react. Similarly in Ireland, in the twentieth century the visual arts have had to react to an unprecedented onslaught from an often arrogant external influence.[2] In each case, therefore, the British and Irish painters have been divided in their aspirations, one section in part fighting a rear guard action in defence of traditional, even native methods and concerns, another, and in both cases the dominant, section adamant in their espousal of Modernism with its evangelistic tendencies. In each case, too, Modernism meant almost solely avant-garde French art.

To begin with the Irish painters were ahead of their British contemporaries in their understanding of the new art, for since the mid-nineteenth century a number of Irish artists had studied and worked in France and had known the Barbizon painters, the Impressionists and Post-Impressionists at first hand. The ideas thus garnered they brought back to Ireland. One of the first Irish painters to work in France was Nathaniel Hone (1831-1917), who went there, to Fontainebleau and Barbizon, in the 1850s. Hone learned to work briskly in a *plein air* manner which contrasted with the narrow academic approach of his fellow-countrymen at the time. Following Hone, Frank O'Meara (1853-88), Sir John Lavery (1856-1941), Walter Osborne (1859-1903) and Roderic O'Conor (1860-1940), for example, all went to France where they obtained a first-hand acquaintance with avant-garde painting, and O'Conor became a friend of Paul Gauguin. O'Meara's *Autumnal Sorrows*, 1878 (no. 29), captures the moody solemnity characteristic of much of the new Realism of the period in France and Osborne's *Cherry Ripe*, 1889 (no. 30), brings something of the same mood to a representation of a Dublin street scene. O'Conor's *View of Pont Aven*, 1899 (no. 31), on the other hand bristles with the spontaneous brushwork and emphasis on the gestural act of painting which came with Post-Impressionism.

Ireland at the *fin de siècle* was in a volatile state. The celebrated Literary Revival was underway and the events which led to the revolutionary period of 1916-21 were beginning to form in certain minds. It is noteworthy that, in this climate, while the literary people often looked inwards, drawing inspiration from their own traditions and having to some extent a political agenda, the best of their contemporaries among the painters looked abroad, to Continental Europe and the new avant-garde which was forming there.

The development of painting in the twentieth century in Ireland, again as in Britain, is in the main a tale of groups of artists coming together for reasons of mutual interest, rather than a story of the work of individual painters of the first rank, although Jack B. Yeats (1871-1957) in Ireland and Francis Bacon (1909-92) in England may be considered exceptions to this rule. In both countries the painters who formed these groups came together principally to oppose what they saw as a reactionary intransigence from the established Academies and other groups. In Ireland the main issue in the early years of the century centred upon the perceived need to create a distinct Irish School of painting, and there were two schools of thought as to how this might be accomplished. Firstly, the more academic painters argued that artists should concentrate their attention, much as their literary contemporaries had done, on those things which were considered to be distinctly Irish - representations of the west, folk festivals, and so on - alas, the stock motifs of Irish identity. But while there was in Ireland a living tradition of folk epic, music and history to which the literary people had been able to turn for inspiration, there was no similar visual tradition. Secondly, however, the avant-garde painters argued that Irish artists should forget about such themes and should instead espouse the ideals of the new art coming from France which they argued was more appropriate to the needs of the new century then at its beginning. Eventually, it was the latter group who won the argument.

As the debate progressed a number of exhibitions of modern painting were arranged and these served to inform a wider audience. Of these exhibitions, the inclusion of twenty-six pictures by James McNeill Whistler - the *enfant terrible* of the art world at the time - at the Dublin Sketching Club in 1884, the *Modern Paintings* show held in Dublin in 1899 and Belfast in 1906, *Works by Post-Impressionist Painters*, Dublin 1911, and *Modern French Pictures*, Dublin 1912, were all seminal events. Yet in the end, paradoxically, the most enduring result of this debate was not a work of art at all but the establishment of an art gallery, namely the Dublin Municipal Gallery of Modern Art,[3] which was established in 1908 largely through the efforts of the picture dealer Hugh (later Sir Hugh) Lane. With the 'Municipal Gallery', as it has always been known, good modern paintings against which Irish artists could measure themselves, were now permanently on view to the public. As has been said, these developments took place on the eve of a revolutionary period in Irish politics, yet little of the turmoil of that time, or the years which followed, found its way into the work of the leading Irish artists.

Besides the issues already mentioned, British and Irish painting at the turn of the century shared certain other points in common; in particular, both were minor schools - although none the less interesting for that - and both were greatly inspired by the native landscape. Moreover in London, as in Dublin, there existed only a handful of galleries and private patronage operated only on a limited scale. In both places the influence of French painting predominated.

Walter Sickert (1860-1942) was the doyen of the British avant-garde. Born in Munich, he had come with his parents to England in 1868. He studied art at the Slade School, London, and under Whistler, but in 1883 visited Paris, where he met Degas, Bonnard, Vuillard and Signac, and thereafter paid regular visits to France. Thus he gained a knowledge of the latest artistic developments at first hand. Sickert settled in London in 1905, a date which is often taken as marking the beginning of Modernism in Britain - it was also the year of Durand-Ruel's comprehensive London show of paintings from Boudin to Cézanne - and for a time his studio in Fitzroy Street became a meeting place for young and progressive painters. Of Sickert's friends and contemporaries, William Rothenstein (1872-1945) had studied in Paris where he knew Degas, Monet and Toulouse-Lautrec; Robert Bevan (1865-1925) had been in Paris and knew Gauguin, and Lucien Pissarro (1863-1944), Camille Pissarro's son, settled in London in 1890 and was an important link between French and English art.

From out of this circle of friends there emerged, in 1907, the Fitzroy Street Group which, focusing on Sickert, Spencer Gore (1878-1914), Harold Gilman (1876-1919), Robert Bevan and Charles Ginner (1878-1952) - artists for whom Post-Impressionism had largely superseded the new orthodoxy of Impressionism - was for a time the centre of the English avant-garde. The Irish painter Paul Henry (1876-1958), who had also been in Paris, was another frequenter of Sickert's circle as on occasions were the writer George Moore and Hugh Lane. In 1908 a number of these artists, including Paul Henry, formed the Allied Artists' Association (AAA) as a sort of English version of the French Salon des Indépendants. Unlike most other groups at the time, the AAA was run on egalitarian lines: no picture was refused admission, works by foreign artists were accepted and the hanging committee was chosen alphabetically. In 1910 Charles Ginner, who earlier in Paris had been influenced by Van Gogh and Gauguin, exhibited with the AAA and thus moved the attention of his associates, in particular Gilman and Gore, towards Post-Impressionism. A year later, in 1911, Ginner, Gilman and Gore formed the influential Camden Town Group, adopting a clearly Modernist aesthetic, developing an interest in colour for its own sake and in terms of subject-matter aiming to paint daily life around them untainted by any picturesque or romantic bias.

While these developments were underway there occurred one of the most seminal exhibitions to have been staged in London this century. Organized by the critic Roger Fry, *Manet and the Post-Impressionists*, opened at the Grafton Galleries in November 1910. For the show Fry gathered together twenty-one pictures by Cézanne, thirty-seven by Gauguin, twenty Van Goghs as well as works by Derain, Matisse, Picasso and others. The exhibition grew notorious, abused as the work of charlatans by the art establishment and sections of the press and misunderstood by the public in general But it gave succour to the Camden Town painters and stiffened their resolve in favour of the new art from France. Later, in 1912, a second Post-Impressionist exhibition was held in London and this included an English section which served to stimulate the more progressive artists and to sharpen the divide between them and their academic colleagues, for whom romanticism and narrative still dominated. Yet despite this divide, one or two of the more academic painters, including the Irishman John Lavery (1856-1941), who adopted a *plein air* approach, and Ambrose McEvoy (1878-1927), who brought an Impressionist-derived wistful spontaneity to his work, managed an accommodation with the new trends, as did Augustus John (1878-1961) and J.D. Innes (1887-1914) and, to some extent, Sickert himself, although he later came to feel uneasy in the face of the avant-garde.

Wyndham Lewis (1882-1957) joined the Camden Town Group in 1911. Lewis, who was a writer as well as a painter, was a restless spirit. He had travelled widely in Europe and was familiar with the avant-garde. In particular, he was influenced by Cubism from which he developed a highly structured art form much indebted to theory, both artistic and socio-political. Such an approach put him to some extent at odds with the other Camden Town painters but drew him to the company of David Bomberg (1890-1957) and William Roberts (1895-1980), both of whom shared similar views, and together they began to work towards a completely non-representational art form. For a time Lewis, Bomberg and Roberts worked with the Omega Workshops, which Roger Fry had established in 1913 to promote better design in furniture, pottery, textiles and furnishings of various kinds, but they soon gave that up to pursue a more rigorous expression and in the process founded the so-called Rebel Art Centre, which had a distinct socio-political dimension to its activities. From this background developed Vorticism, a non-representational art form which was arguably the most vital English contribution to modern art. Vorticism espoused a dynamic aesthetic, sharing much in common with Italian Futurism, although it was less polemically determined than the latter. The philosopher T.E. Hume, who worked with Lewis and company, set out their credentials when he wrote in 1914 that their moves towards abstraction would (as with Futurism) 'culminate, not so much in ... simple geometrical forms ... but in the more complicated ones associated ... with the idea of machinery'.[4] The publication by the group in July 1914 of the first issue of *Blast*, a short-lived paper in which they set out their aims and lambasted those with whom they disagreed, cemented their affinity with the Futurists. As Hume prophesied, however, pictures such as Lewis' *The Crowd*, 1914-15, Bomberg's *The mud bath*, 1914, or *In the hold*, 1913-14 (all Tate Gallery), were to be amongst the most dynamic works by an English painter done this century. Alas, the outbreak of war in August 1914 brought these developments largely to a halt, for many of the protagonists, like others, soon found themselves fighting on the western front.

In 1913 yet another formation took place when a number of the Camden Town painters joined with Lewis' colleagues to form the London Group. The new Group was in essence an exhibition platform for those who found few such opportunities elsewhere, a situation which became worse after the outbreak of the war. Through the London Group - which was to have a long and distinguished history - Mark Gertler (1892-1939), Stanley Spencer (1891-1939) and Paul Nash (1889-1946) all came to the fore. Gertler came from the Jewish East End of London and in his work portrayed life there with great intensity. His *Merry-go-round*, 1916 (Ben Uri Art Gallery), an important picture from the period, however, has a universality in its condemnation of the senselessness of war. Spencer was a loner. Brought up in Cookham-on-Thames he expressed an intensely religious devotion in his art which, although it has a certain naivety, still impresses with its conviction. His experiences as a medical orderly during the war profoundly affected his outlook into the 1930s and beyond. Paul Nash was appointed an Official War Artist and produced some of the most hauntingly memorable images of wanton destruction - *We are Making a New World*, 1918, or *The Menin Road*, 1918-19 (both Imperial War Museum, London), for example - to emanate from that time. By the end of the war, or shortly afterwards, the London Group had come to represent the best of that which was considered avant-garde in British art and although it then lost something of its pioneering edge, it provided a seed bed for those who would later come to prominence in the 1920s and 1930s.

The first major group of artists to establish themselves in Dublin was the Society of Dublin Painters which Paul Henry and a few contemporaries founded in 1920.[5] Henry had been a student in Paris, where he met Whistler, and had absorbed himself in the avant-garde there before settling in London where he frequented Sickert s circle and joined the Allied Artists' Association. In 1910 he returned to Ireland, going to Achill Island off the coast of Connemara, and there he remained for almost a decade before settling in Dublin in 1919. Henry quickly became disenchanted with the reactionary policies pursued by the art establishment in Dublin - principally with the Royal Hibernian Academy - and as a result he established the Society of Dublin Painters as a forum where those with an interest in the avant-garde could exhibit their work free from the selection procedures of the Academy. The Society of Dublin Painters was modelled on Sickert's Fitzroy Street Group. They took rooms and organized regular one-man exhibitions of members' work as well as a group show each spring and autumn. Before long the 'Dublin Painters', as they became known, represented all the most progressive painters working in Ireland. That the Society should have come into being and thrived in such a revolutionary period - the aftermath of the Easter Rising of 1916, the Anglo-Irish war and the subsequent Treaty of 1921, the establishment of the Irish Free State, 1922, and the subsequent Irish Civil War - is surprising in itself, but more surprising perhaps is the fact that these events had little perceptible effect on the work of its members who included, in its first decade, Paul Henry and his wife Grace (1868-1953), Harry Clarke (1889-1931), E.M.O'R. Dickey (1894-1977), Letitia Hamilton (1880-1964), Mainie Jellett (1897-1944), Charles Lamb (1893-1964), Clare Marsh (1874-1923), Mary Swanzy (1882-1978) and Jack B. Yeats. For two decades the Dublin Painters were the most influential body of painters in Ireland with an interest in the avant-garde. Alas, however, their modernism was in the main confined to the influence of French painting and in particular to a sort of watered-down Impressionism and, later, Fauvism which by the 1920s had lost the thrust of innovation. Only Mainie Jellett and, to a lesser extent, Mary Swanzy, took any notice of more recent developments such as Cubism, and Jellett eventually developed a fully fleged abstraction of considerable worth, while Cecil Salkeld (1904-69) was the only Irish artist of his generation to take any cognizance of the New Objectivity movement which began in Germany in the 1920s. Jack B. Yeats, the major Irish painter of his generation, had only a brief association with the Dublin Painters. As in all respects of his life, he pursued his own path, his interests to begin with being those of an observer of the Ireland in which he lived, as *Bachelor's Walk, In Memory*, 1915 and *A Westerly Wind*, 1921, (both private collections), or *The Island Funeral*, 1923 (Sligo Museum and Art Gallery), for example illustrate; while from the late 1920s onwards, in compositions like *A Race in Hy Brazil*, 1937 (Allied Irish Bank, Dublin) or *On Through the Silent Lands*, 1951 (Ulster Museum), he concerned himself increasingly with esoteric issues to do with personal emotions, even the nature of life, all rendered with a strong universality.

In the 1920s and 1930s in Ireland there emerged a strong body of landscape painters. By the mid-to-late twenties Paul Henry was seen as the leading painter of this group, pictures such as his *Lakeside Cottages*, c.1929-30 (Hugh Lane Municipal Gallery of Modern Art, Dublin), exerting an enormous influence on the scene, but other artists who were influenced by him but who each developed a recognizable and cogent style of their own, include James Humbert Craig (1878-1944) and Frank McKelvey (1895-1974), whose *Evening, Ballycastle* (no. 32), of about 1924, is typical of much that they produced. These painters brought a new degree of Realism, of verisimilitude, to their treatment of the Irish landscape and evolved a view of that landscape which, even with the passage of time, is still persuasive to us today. Henry, Craig and McKelvey were all northerners, but their contemporaries in the south of Ireland included, amongst others, Dermod O'Brien (1865-1945), Sean Keating (1889-1977) and Maurice MacGonigal (1900-79). O'Brien, after studying for a time in the late 1880s and early 1890s in Belgium and France, returned home and established himself as a portrait painter, a genre which he practised with much success throughout his long career. He was also a competent landscapist, working in a *plein air* manner which derives some influence from Walter Osborne and other of his early contemporaries. O'Brien was for many years president of the Royal Hibernian Academy and as such was a prominent figure in many aspects of the art scene in Ireland. Keating and MacGonigal were, with Jack B. Yeats, the foremost Irish painters to concern themselves with the social policies of the new Ireland, as it developed in the years following 1922. But whereas Yeats was interested in human issues and often momentous events, Keating and MacGonigal were preoccupied with the land itself, bringing to their work an acute sense of tradition, of history, combined with an evocation of ownership of the land, an issue which had dominated much of recent Irish history.

Viewed overall the development of Irish painting in the years between the wars was of a constant pull between those who espoused Modernist ideas emanating in the main from France - Georgina Moutray Kyle's *The Lifting of the Fog at the Gasworks, Belfast* (no. 33), c.1926, is a good example of this - and those who pursued a more reactionary path, but one which involved itself with the new State as it began to evolve.

In British painting, on the other hand, the inter-war years were a period of consolidation by the generation who had come to the fore before 1914, although the time also saw the development of abstract painting, notably from the hands of Ben Nicholson (1894-1982), Graham Sutherland (1903-80), Ivon Hitchens (1893-1979), Paul Nash (1889-1946) - who had been active before the First World War - Christopher Wood (1901-30) and John Piper (1903-92). These are the names which dominated the scene till the outbreak of the Second World War and after.

Nicholson, Hitchens, Piper and Wood were drawn together through membership of the progressive Seven & Five Society[6] which was established in the late 1920s. Others prominent in it were the sculptors Henry Moore (1898-1986) and Barbara Hepworth (1903-75) and the Irish artists Evie Hone (1894-1955) and Mainie Jellett also exhibited there. By the early 1930s the Seven & Five Society had become a platform for the new abstraction and Ben Nicholson was its most distinctive proponent. Nicholson's principal subject-matter stemmed from landscape and still life, both of which he treated in a highly simplified but geometrically structured manner of great subtlety, eventually evolving a completely abstract form. *Painting 1935* (no. 34), exemplifies this development and illustrates the Platonic nature[7] of Nicholson's work. More or less contemporary with this picture Nicholson began to make relief works, exploring in three dimensions the same sort of formal relationships. But whereas Nicholson approached abstraction by way of geometrical forms, his contemporary Graham Sutherland developed a sort of organic abstraction based on the study of natural forms, as can be seen, for example, in his *Gorse on a Sea Wall*, of 1939 (no. 35). Nicholson and Sutherland, in company with Piper, Hitchens, Nash and Hepworth, represented the cutting edge of British art on the eve of the Second World War, although others associated with Unit One, which Paul Nash had established in 1933, were moving in a broadly similar direction.

The Unit One artists espoused no common aesthetic, but were rather linked by what Nash described as 'a quality of mind ... a truly contemporary spirit',[8] and Herbert Read in a book about the Unit defined this spirit as an abandonment of the 'truth to nature' approach to painting, of historical precedents, and of imagination explored apart from literature or metaphysics.[9] The Unit put together an exhibition of works which toured Britain in 1934 and which went to Belfast too. As a result of this a group of sympathizers in Belfast established the 'Ulster Unit', with broadly the same aesthetic as their English counterparts. Of the members of the Ulster Unit, which was short-lived and held only one exhibition, in Belfast in December 1934, Colin Middleton (1910-83) and John Luke (1906-75) were the most adventurous. Luke had recently returned to Belfast from London where he had been a student at the Slade School and had begun to develop the severely formalized style for which, in pictures such as *The Fox*, 1937 (Ulster Museum), or *The Three Dancers*, 1945 (no. 37) - the latter composition shows his style at its most extreme - he is best known. He was thus excited at the prospect of promoting a Modernist style in Ulster art. Meanwhile Middleton was moving towards his own form of abstraction with a mildly Surrealist edge. Even though it was short-lived, the Ulster Unit, in the words of its 1934 exhibition catalogue, comprised a body of artists alert to European influence, 'while that influence is still real and vital'; they were, too, the only artists in Ireland at the time to espouse corporately a meaningful aesthetic based on contemporary trends.

Although Surrealism had been a major - perhaps the dominating - movement in Europe in the 1920s and early 1930s its influence only really made an impact in Britain with the *International Surrealist Exhibition* held in London in 1936, although Paul Nash, John Banting (1902-72), the Irish sculptor F.E. McWilliam (1909-72), who was living in London, and others had all made Surrealist-type works, often based on *objects trouvés*. However, the Surrealist exhibition (which John Luke chanced to visit), plus the associated readings, 'happenings', political demonstrations and other events, focused attention in Britain on Surrealism, although the 'real' politics of the late 1930s and the outbreak of war in 1939 soon led to the demise of the movement.

The outbreak of war naturally disrupted the art scene in Britain, although in the south of Ireland (a neutral country, that is, apart from Northern Ireland) things were a little different. As we have seen, throughout the 1920s and 1930s Irish artists had been split between those who advocated Modernism and those who advocated a return to a more definite - if always unexplained - Irish subject-matter. With the European war, however, several Irish artists - Norah McGuinness (1903-80), Patrick Hennessy (1915-81), and Louis le Brocquy (b.1916) amongst them - who had spent the thirties abroad returned home and, naturally, brought support to those with an avant-garde agenda. From these developments there emerged in 1943 the *Irish Exhibition of Living Art*, which became an annual event representing all that was progressive in Irish art. Le Brocquy and Mainie Jellett provided the driving force behind the new exhibition, which caused a considerable stir in an otherwise conservative environment. Of the generation of artists which the *Living Art* exhibitions introduced to the Irish scene Norah McGuinness, Colin Middleton, George Campbell (1917-79), Nevill Johnson (b.1911), Dan O'Neill (1920-74) and Gerard Dillon (1916-71) all came from Northern Ireland, and Le Brocquy, Nano Reid (1910-81), Anne Yeats (b.1919) and a few others came from the south. Together they shaped the course of

Irish art till the 1960s. Middleton's 1946 composition, *Our Lady of Bikini* (private collection), and Johnson's *Landscape Rock Pool*, c.1950 (Hugh Lane Municipal Gallery of Modern Art, Dublin), both poignant comments on the new atomic age, and Le Brocquy's *A Family*, 1951 (Néstlé Italiana SPA, Milan), a reflection on the isolation of the individual within society, are all memorable images from the period. Gerard Dillon was one of the most important of these painters, his subject-matter often being drawn from rural life, although he frequently brought an urban sophistication to what pretended to be a simple environment. His *Yellow Bungalow* (no. 38) illustrates the point. The notion of solitariness (as with Le Brocquy) which is evident in it, the bird's eye view, narrative format and hint of Symbolism all betraying a sophisticated mind at work.

Most of the leading figures in British art had by the end of the Second World War adopted a Modernist aesthetic. Ivon Hitchens, who of course had been active in the pre-war years, Roger Hilton (1911-75) and William Scott (1913-89), who was an Ulsterman, were amongst the most progressive in their ideas. Hitchens was mainly a landscape and flower painter. In 1934 he had contributed to the exhibition *Objective Abstractions* at the Zwemmer Gallery, London - the Belfast painter Tom Carr (b.1909) had also shown on that occasion - joining a number of artists who, while embracing the avant-garde in terms of subtly juxtaposed planes and colours, nevertheless retained a representational element in their work. This was a line of development with which Hitchens continued till the end of his career and in works such as *Spring in Autumn*, 1967 (no. 41), he achieved great poetic sensitivity towards landscape and its moods. Roger Hilton, on the other hand, embraced a more thorough-going abstraction, as his *January 1962* (no. 40) illustrates, but his art nevertheless remained rooted in the sexuality of the human figure, which he depicted with great sensuousness and pathos. William Scott spent almost his entire career in England, but due to his Ulster upbringing he retained links with Ireland so that he can be seen in the context of both British and Irish painting. Throughout his career he derived much stimulus from still life objects as subject-matter - in particular pots and pans found in the kitchen - his early works retaining a strong representational element which, in time, gave way to abstraction, such as *White with Red Lines* (no. 39), in which he manipulated these familiar forms to lie flat upon the picture plane so that they are read solely as shapes juxtaposed one with another. In company with other painters such as Patrick Heron (b.1920), Peter Lanyon (1918-64) and the colony of St Ives painters, Hitchens, Hilton and Scott were amongst the most forceful of the British painters to face the challenge of American Abstract

Expressionism and Colour Field Painting which burst upon the British public in the late 1950s. The major British painter of this generation, however, was Francis Bacon, who was born in Dublin of English parents. Something of a loner, Bacon pursued a path to which people - in reality the 'human condition' - were the central theme.

Amongst the major achievements of British art in the 1960s and 1970s were the development of Pop Art and Op Art. David Hockney (b. 1937), Peter Blake (b. 1932) and Joe Tilson (b. 1928) were the most influential painters associated with the former movement, while Bridget Riley (b. 1931), Peter Sedgley (b. 1930) and Jeffrey Steele (b. 1931) belong to the latter. These developments, however, are beyond the scope of this essay, although influences from the former can be seen in Stephen McKenna's *Maritime Still Life*, 1993 (no. 43). The 1980s and early 1990s in Britain, as elsewhere, saw a return to representational painting which, by the mid '90s, had become the dominant force. The same might be said of Irish painting, although in Ireland abstraction had never firmly taken root, a more traditional imagery having endured even the revolutions of the 1960s. T.P. Flanagan (b. 1929), a landscapist, is one of the most important Irish painters of his generation, his *Gortahork (2)*, 1969 (no. 42), illustrating the way in which he often fragments the landscape in terms of making one conscious of both the surface and the sub-structure - and, literally, the historical past - of the terrain. Flanagan's work is always concise in concept and precise in execution, his brushwork at times having a calligraphic quality which imparts a literary feel to it. Basil Blackshaw (b. 1932), an exact contemporary of Flanagan, is more Expressionist in approach. He too is a painter of landscapes but people and animals are his real interest. His work is full of emotion, with a strong sense of 'place' which at times gives an autobiographical feel to it. The *Barn (Blue II)*, 1993 (no. 45), is a good example of his recent development and, as is evident in it, he has a finely honed sense of colour.

In contrast to the immediacy of their influence in the literary sphere the Ulster 'Troubles' of the past twenty-five years were relatively slow to impact upon the visual arts. Of course many clichéd images did appear and many artists felt a compulsion to come to terms with the Troubles in their work, but not always with the best results. Joseph McWilliams (b. 1938), who first came to prominence in the late 1960s, however, has consistently made the Troubles his concern - he is an observer, not a commentator - and has produced a substantial body of work which is of great socio-historical interest and importance. His *The Governors of Anguilla, Gibraltar, the Caymen Islands and the Last Governor of Northern Ireland* (no. 44), painted in 1989, refers in a broad sweep to some of the issues inherent not just in the Northern Irish situation but in post-coloniality in general. It is, however, principally with the younger generation in Ulster, with Dermot Seymour (b. 1956), the Delargy brothers, John Kindness (b. 1951) and a few others, that the Troubles have, sadly, a less exceptional, more permanent place in their perceptions. Of British painters, Ken Howard (b. 1932) and John Keane (b. 1954) have also made memorable images of the Ulster crisis, the former's *Ulster Crucifixion*, 1978 (Ulster Museum), having a strong element of the universal in its use of imagery.

Dr S. B. Kennedy
Head of Fine and Applied Art

References

1. Richard Shone, *The Century of Change: British Painting Since 1900* (Oxford, 1977).

2. For a detailed account of the Irish reaction to Modernism see S.B. Kennedy, *Irish Art and Modernism 1880-1950* (Belfast, 1991).

3. Now the Hugh Lane Municipal Gallery of Modern Art.

4. Hume, quoted in Shone, op. cit., p.19.

5. For a full discussion of the founding of the Society of Dublin Painters see Kennedy, op cit., pp.18-46.

6. So called because the original (1919) membership comprised seven painters and five sculptors; the membership, however, soon increased beyond these limitations.

7. Plato's Theory of Forms is evoked by Nicholson's juxtaposition of 'pure' geometrical shapes.

8. Paul Nash, letter to *The Times*, London 2 June 1933.

9. Herbert Read (ed.), *Unit 1: The Modern Movement in English Architecture, Painting and Sculpture* (London, 1934), p.12.

Four Centuries of Irish History

The history of Ireland has always been closely interwoven with that of the British Isles as a whole, but particularly so over the past four centuries - the period covered by this exhibition. For half of that time, however, the whole of Ireland was in theory a separate kingdom, with its own parliament and laws, its own currency, its own units of measurement (Irish acres, Irish miles) and the distinctive local division of land known as the townland which is still in common use. In more recent times, for most of the island, separate government, laws and currency have been restored, in an independence much more real than was ever enjoyed by the so-called independent Irish parliament of the late eighteenth century. In the north of Ireland, however, the British connection has continued, though subject in recent times to increasing challenge and change.

The roots of this division lie deep in the past. To go back no farther than the early years of the seventeenth century, the long-drawn-out English conquest of Ireland was completed during the closing years of the reign of Queen Elizabeth I (died 1603) by the defeat of Hugh O'Neill, Earl of Tyrone and other Gaelic chieftains of Ulster who were his allies. A few years later in 1607, O'Neill, O'Donnell, Maguire and others fled to Europe, from which they never returned. This Flight of the Earls enabled the English government in Dublin to declare their lands forfeit to the crown and to introduce a scheme of plantation which would put an end to traditional Irish society, a society that was regarded as backward and barbaric. The official Plantation of Ulster aimed to establish a colony of English and Scottish Protestants on the confiscated lands in west and central Ulster; private schemes in the east of the province, in Counties Antrim and Down, which already had close ties with Scotland, achieved the same effect there. The Ulster plantation was by far the largest and most ambitious of all such schemes and did in the end succeed in establishing a large permanent population of English and Scottish Protestants in the north-east of Ireland. Elsewhere in the country, the vast majority of the population remained essentially Irish and Catholic.

The new settlers transformed Ulster by building towns, developing trade and commerce, improving agriculture, clearing large areas of woodland and introducing up-to-date architecture - in short, by modernising society. The largest of the undertakers, as the leading planters were called because they undertook to fulfil the conditions of the Plantation, was a consortium of London merchant companies, which gave its name to County Londonderry and a new walled city at the mouth of the River Foyle. In many ways the

Plantation in the north of Ireland was like contemporary schemes of settlement in North America. Unlike many of the native peoples of America, however, the previous inhabitants were not exterminated by the settlers; instead they remained as tenants or labourers, subordinate as before but to new masters. Some of their old chieftain families also survived, for a time at least, as English-style landowners of reduced estates, but most of these subsequently lost their lands when they rebelled against the new order in 1641. One outstanding survivor was the head of the MacDonnell clan, who became Earl of Antrim and remained the greatest landowner in that county despite also retaining his Catholic faith. The estate was twice confiscated and twice restored in the century that followed the Plantation and the remains of it are still in the family's possession. MacDonnell's chief opponent was Arthur Chichester, a soldier from Devon who played a major part in the Plantation as King James's deputy in Ireland and who acquired huge amounts of land both in the official scheme in County Donegal - from which later Chichesters derived their titles of earls and marquesses of Donegall (the seventeenth-century spelling) - and also in County Antrim, including the castle and lands of Belfast. Arthur Chichester once declared that he would rather labour with his hands in the Plantation of Ulster than dance or play in that of Virginia!

The 1641 rebellion, which for a time almost destroyed the Plantation, led to years of confused fighting throughout Ireland, in which armies of Catholic Irish, Catholic Old English (as the descendants of earlier English settlers were called), Protestant New English and Scots fought in shifting alliances which reflected the civil war in England between King Charles I and his parliament. The contest between Cavaliers and Roundheads ended in the defeat of the king and his execution in 1649. Parliament then turned its attention to Ireland, to which it dispatched its victorious general Oliver Cromwell and his New Model Army. Following Cromwell's devastating campaign, during which the royalist garrisons of Drogheda and Wexford were put to the sword when they refused to surrender, most of the property still belonging to Catholic landowners in the provinces of Ulster, Leinster and Munster (along with that of leading Protestant royalists) was confiscated. The displaced Catholic proprietors and their families, those who did not go abroad, were transported to the province of Connaught in the far west and settled there. Their estates were granted to Cromwellian officers and supporters of Parliament.

When Charles II was restored to the throne in 1660 this wholesale transfer of Irish land was only partly reversed, the new Cromwellian proprietors keeping most of what they had gained, to the great disappointment of the previous owners. A generation later, when

Charles's brother and successor, the Catholic monarch James II (who reigned 1685-8), needed the support of his Irish Catholic subjects during the Revolution of 1688-9, the Restoration settlement was briefly overthrown, only to be confirmed once more following James's defeat at the Battle of the Boyne in 1690 by William of Orange (William III), his Protestant son-in-law. Further confiscations ensued and, though some of the land forfeited was eventually restored, it has been reckoned that by the beginning of the eighteenth century no more than fourteen per cent of Irish land remained in the hands of Catholic landowners (the proportion in 1688 had been twenty-two per cent).

In the century after 1600, then, the ownership of most of the land of Ireland changed. Below the small landowning class, however, most of those who actually occupied and tilled the soil remained Irish and Catholic. The exception to this was the north-east, where Protestants of British descent were not only numerous but also to be found in all ranks of society. The majority were adherents of the Presbyterian church rather than the Church of Ireland and indeed were hostile to bishops and the episcopalian system. Yet the Church of Ireland as the only official church was endowed by the state and the entire population of the country - Catholics and Dissenters as well as members of the established church - had to pay tithes to support it.

William III himself was tolerant in matters of religion. His Irish parliament, however, was determined to ensure that there would be no further challenges to the ascendancy of the Protestants. (The name applied at that time only to members of the Church of Ireland; Presbyterians and others of the reformed faith were known as Dissenters). During the reigns of William and his successor Queen Anne (who reigned 1702-14) it passed a series of laws which limited the political and social power of Catholics - the penal laws, as they are collectively known. To prevent their raising another army, Catholics were forbidden to bear arms without a licence or own a horse worth more than £5 (that is, a cavalry mount). They were also forbidden to send their children abroad to be educated (and were likewise prohibited from running schools at home). Bishops and members of religious orders were expelled and parish clergy, though permitted to remain and work, had to be registered with the authorities and give security for their good behaviour. Already excluded (by English law) from sitting in Parliament, Catholics were effectively also excluded from voting or from holding office in local government and were not allowed to become solicitors.

The penal laws, in fact, were aimed particularly at Catholic landowners, since land was the chief source of wealth, power and status. From that point of view, the statute which hit hardest was an Act of 1704, under which Catholics could not acquire land from Protestants and could not transmit their estates to their eldest son by will; instead, the property had to be divided equally amongst all the sons, unless one of them converted to the Church of Ireland, in which case he could claim the entire inheritance. Faced with a choice between keeping their faith and losing their land and social status, most Catholic landowners converted and in due course their estates became Protestant land. By 1780, it was reckoned, only five per cent remained in Catholic ownership. Little or no attempt was made to convert the Catholic population as a whole, however; the aim of the Protestant ruling class was to reduce it to political impotence. The penal laws against Catholicism as a religion were seldom vigorously enforced and many became dead letters as time went on, but the intention they expressed at the time and the fact of their continued existence on the statute book left a great deal of bitterness.

Catholics were not the only victims. So too were Protestant Dissenters, mostly Presbyterians, who had played a prominent part in achieving the Williamite victory. By the late seventeenth century the Presbyterians amounted in number to more than half of the Protestants of Ulster and probably nearly half of those in the whole country. Before 1691 they had been alternately tolerated and harassed, their clergy receiving a salary - the *regium donum* or royal gift - from the crown but their attempts to establish new congregations were opposed by local magistrates and their rites attacked or undermined by the ecclesiastical courts of the official church. (Presbyterian marriages, for example, were treated as invalid). For some years after 1691 their position improved. During most of Anne's reign, however, Dissenters suffered active discrimination. The anti-popery Act passed by the Irish parliament in 1704, by requiring all holders of public office to qualify themselves by taking the sacrament in the Church of Ireland, effectively excluded Presbyterians as well as Catholics from official positions and in 1714 the *regium donum* was actually suspended. The Church of Ireland bishops and their supporters detested the Presbyterians, not so much because of their religious beliefs as because Presbyterianism, with its system of synods, presbyteries, ministers and lay elders, was not only anti-episcopalian in particular but opposed to hierarchies in general - and therefore potentially subversive of a society where landowners expected obedience from their social inferiors.

After 1714, when George of Hanover ascended the throne as George I and thus secured the Protestant succession, governments discouraged the Church of Ireland from harassing Presbyterians or from enforcing the letter of the law against their marriages. In 1719 the Irish parliament even passed a limited toleration act. The religious test in the penal statute of 1704 remained, however, and for most of the eighteenth century continued to exclude Dissenters from the share in local government that their numbers and growing commercial wealth should have entitled them to. And, since Anglican landowners were thus able to control not only the county seats but also the borough seats, whose holders made up the bulk of the Irish House of Commons, all attempts to repeal the religious test for Presbyterians were defeated. Like the Catholics, Dissenters were left in no position to challenge the privileges of the Church of Ireland and the Anglican upper class. Thus was established and maintained the system that came to be called the Protestant ascendancy in church and state.

One result of Presbyterian dissatisfaction with life in Ireland in the eighteenth century was a steady tide of emigration. This was the source of most of the early wave of Irish immigrants to North America. Religious discontent was one motive for going. Another was economic hardship. In consequence, some who had flocked into Ulster in the 1690s stayed barely one generation before departing again for America. The connection, once established, encouraged others later. These were the ancestors of the Scotch-Irish. They or their descendants were to supply the American colonists with a number of their leaders in the War of Independence and the United States with several of its presidents. The Declaration of Independence, the original of which is in the handwriting of Charles Thompson of Maghera, County Londonderry and whose first signatory was John Hancock, whose ancestors came from County Down, was printed by John Dunlap, who had learned his trade in Strabane, County Tyrone. During the previous half-century, at least 100,000 people and probably many more had gone from Ulster to America. By the end of the century a quarter of a million Americans - about one-sixth of the entire European population of the United States - claimed to be descended from the Scotch-Irish.

After the upheavals of the seventeenth century, the eighteenth was a period of prolonged peace and growing prosperity. The prosperity, however, was distributed very unevenly. In the countryside, rising agricultural prices encouraged landowners to raise rents, which led to a number of agrarian campaigns of violence amongst tenants. Amongst large land owners, greater wealth was reflected in the building of fine houses and the beautification of estates. One of the finest and earliest of these new mansions was Castletown in County Kildare, built for William Conolly, the Speaker of the Irish parliament, in the 1720s. In the 1730s and 40s the most fashionable architect was the German-born Richard Castle or Cassel, who designed both Russborough and Powerscourt in County Wicklow amongst others. The finest country house in the north of Ireland and the finest late-Georgian house anywhere in Ireland - Castlecoole in County Fermanagh - was built for the Earl of Belmore in the 1790s to the designs of James Wyatt. In fact, the eighteenth century was the golden age of the great house in Ireland.

As well as these country palaces, the leading Anglo-Irish families also built town houses in Dublin, where they lived when parliament was in session. The grandest of these was Leinster House, now the seat of the Irish parliament, which was built for the Fitz Geralds, earls of Kildare and (from 1766) dukes of Leinster, by Richard Castle. Incidentally, Castle's design was later adapted by the Irish-born architect James Hoban for the presidential mansion in Washington, DC - the building known as the White House, after it was painted to cover traces of a fire started by fellow Irishman Robert Ross, the British general who briefly occupied Washington in 1814. The town houses of the aristocracy and the less imposing but still substantial dwellings of the gentry, merchants and professional classes who swelled the growing population of Dublin, provided the city with many elegant streets and squares. It also acquired some of its finest public buildings, notably the old Parliament House (now the Bank of Ireland) on College Green, the facade of Trinity College opposite, the Custom House and the Four Courts (both by the architect James Gandon). Even the crass developments of recent years have not entirely succeeded in destroying the splendours of this once beautiful Georgian city.

Lower in the social scale than the gentry, a number of manufacturers and merchants grew wealthy on the profits of industry and trade. Brewing, for example, made the fortune of the Leeson family in the early eighteenth century, so much so that Joseph Leeson's son - the builder of Russborough, which he filled with works of art purchased in Italy - became Earl of Milltown. Later, brewing also made the fortune of the Guinness family. The linen trade, especially in the north, created a comfortable middle class of dealers and bleachers, as well as providing work for spinners and weavers in their humble homes. Fortunes were made likewise in the provision trade; Cork, for example, had a famous butter market. Overseas trade made fortunes for merchants in Dublin and Belfast as well as Cork. In many cases, visitors remarked, the profits of trade and industry were invested in land rather than ploughed back into the family firm; every successful tradesman seemed to want to become (or at least make his son) a gentleman. Yet for much of the century the squires and squireens who formed the backbone of the Protestant ascendancy in the countryside were scarcely admirable models for emulation. Their rough manners and philistine tastes were later recalled by Sir Jonah Barrington, who famously categorised them into three classes, in ascending order of gentility - half-mounted gentlemen, gentlemen every inch of them and gentlemen to the backbone. Hunting and hard drinking occupied most of their time, along with gambling and duelling, until society became more refined and these hard goers became the stuff of historical fiction, as in Maria Edgeworth's *Castle Rackrent* (1800), the first novel of this well-known Irish author.

Politically, the closing decades of the eighteenth century became increasingly disturbed as, under the influence of liberal ideas from America and France, the status quo was increasingly challenged. The sequence of events began when most of the military garrison in Ireland was withdrawn to fight the rebellious American colonists, leaving the country open to possible invasion by the colonists' ally, France. In 1778 the American privateer John Paul Jones actually captured a Royal Navy ship in Belfast Lough. The citizens of Belfast immediately raised two companies of Volunteers, an example quickly followed elsewhere. All over Ireland, Volunteers put on uniform, armed themselves and drilled enthusiastically. Fortunately, they never had to face the French. Instead, they took to politics and became a Protestant middle-class pressure group, demanding that Ireland be enabled to trade freely with the British Empire and that the Irish parliament have the right to make its own laws, without the need for English approval. Both requests were conceded by 1782. The Volunteers then demanded a reform of parliament itself. This proved more difficult and their influence soon petered out.

The outbreak of the French Revolution in 1789 led to a revival of agitation. Liberals everywhere welcomed the Revolution, at least in its early years. Northern Presbyterians were particularly enthusiastic. But the liberals soon divided on the question of whether - and if so when - the Catholics should be emancipated. In 1791 the more radical amongst them established societies of United Irishmen to press for equal and democratic rights for all. These views were expounded with particular success in a Belfast newspaper, the *Northern Star*. The growing excesses of the Revolution (Louis XVI and Marie Antoinette were executed in 1793) and France's declaration of war on England dampened the ardour of the more cautious reformers, however, and strengthened the resolve of an alarmed Irish government, which presently forbade reform meetings and Volunteer parades and then banned the United Irishmen. Many radicals drew back at this point, but others organised in secret (or what they thought was secret; the movement was actually riddled with informers) and plotted to overthrow the government, with military assistance from France. The government made concessions to Catholics on the one hand whilst on the other, suspected conspirators and their supporters were disarmed and maltreated by the military. A French expedition, under one of the Revolution's best young generals, Hoche, actually arrived off County Cork in December 1796 but was prevented from landing by stormy weather. In 1798 most of the leaders of the United Irishmen in Dublin were arrested. Risings in the south-east (largely Catholic) and the north-east (largely Presbyterian) went ahead but were unco-ordinated and lacked aid from France. Too little, too late and too remote to make a difference, a French army landed in County Mayo and was soon rounded up. Afterwards, the Irish parliament - still as corrupt and unrepresentative as ever - was persuaded to vote for its own dissolution and pass the Act of Union of 1800, by which Ireland became part of the United Kingdom.

The Union got off to a bad start so far as Irish Catholics were concerned when George III was persuaded that it would be contrary to his coronation oath to grant them full civil rights, a measure which his prime minister, William Pitt the younger, had intended should happen. Various attempts were made in the British parliament during the years that followed, but by the time of the King's death in 1820 nothing had been done. At this point Daniel O'Connell, a leading Irish Catholic lawyer, launched the great campaign of popular agitation which not only brought about emancipation in 1829 but in the process created the first successful mass democratic movement in British history. O'Connell's victory was achieved through the use of the Catholic parochial system and with the enthusiastic support of most of the parish clergy (who collected the rent, the numerous modest contributions which supported the campaign). As a result, as one writer puts it: '[O'Connell] set the tone for Irish nationalism thereafter: overwhelmingly Catholic, strong on communal solidarity, populist, localist - and careful not to offend the priests' (Richard Killeen, *A Short History of Ireland*, 1994, p.47).

Pressure by O'Connell and his followers in parliament during the 1830s combined with an unpleasant tithe war in the Irish countryside to bring about reform of the tithe system in 1838. Thereafter O'Connell turned to his second great objective, the repeal of the Union, using mass pressure in a series of monster meetings attended by hundreds of thousands of people at different venues throughout the country - except in Ulster, which he scarcely visited and knew little about. The Union had proved to be good for business in Belfast and the north and few of the descendants of the Presbyterian rebels of 1798 wanted repeal. The government kept its nerve, O'Connell backed down when a monster meeting near Dublin was banned and after a spell in prison he died early in 1847.

By this time the country was in the grip of the great potato famine, which began with the sudden and complete failure of the crop in the autumn of 1845. The disaster occured on such a scale because of a combination of factors: the population of Ireland had exploded to over eight million in a comparatively short time; a high proportion of the people were poor farmers or labourers dependent on the potato alone for food; most of Ireland (with the sole exception of the north-east) had not undergone the kind of industrial revolution which brought alternative work and wages to other parts of the United Kingdom; and against all experience and expectation, the potato failed for several years in succession. The government at Westminster coped reasonably well with the crisis in its early stages, but when a new administration, with a doctrinaire aversion to interfering with the workings of the market, took office, less help was forthcoming at the very time when it was most needed. The majority of deaths during the Famine were the result of disease on weakened constitutions rather than actual starvation, but the effect was the same. Private charity and the efforts of relief organisations could not prevent something like a million deaths. Another million fled the country, many to Britain, more to North America, an exodus which was to continue for a long time. More than three-quarters of a million went to the United States in the 1840s, almost a million in the 1850s; between 1850 and 1930 more than four million went to America alone, not to mention substantial numbers to Australia and elsewhere in the British Empire. Most of these emigrants were Catholics and many took with them bitter memories of British rule.

Post-Famine Ireland remained a predominantly agricultural economy, at a time when it suited the United Kingdom government to abandon protective tariffs for agriculture in order to import cheap food to feed its industrial cities, the source of most of its wealth. Belfast, on the contrary, grew and prospered as never before or since, first on linen (now produced by power-driven machinery rather than by hand), then on shipbuilding, heavy engineering, ropemaking and tobacco. In many respects it was more like Glasgow or Liverpool than any other Irish city. Its industrial and commercial growth attracted many Catholics and others from rural areas, into a town which had hitherto been distinctly Protestant in character. The newcomers tended to settle in particular areas of the city and sectarian tensions between Protestant and Catholic ghetto dwellers were wont to break out at election time or during Orange parades. Riots became common and, as nationalists and unionists became more and more divided, increasingly serious. The success of a new political leader on the nationalist side, Charles Stewart Parnell, who in the 1880s almost achieved Home Rule for Ireland through an alliance with the Liberal prime minister William

Gladstone, led to the formation of the Ulster Unionist party, whose supporters feared not only that Home Rule might mean Rome Rule but that Irish industry would be ruined by a government representing farmers. This growing crisis reached a climax in the years immediately before the First World War, when a Home Rule Bill was actually passed. The Unionists, defying the will of Parliament, organised a provisional government and armed themselves to resist. The issue was shelved for the duration when war broke out in Europe in 1914 and large numbers of Irishmen from both sides volunteered to fight against Germany, perishing in droves in the terrible trench warfare on the Western Front.

Whilst Irishmen thus became increasingly divided along lines of politics and religion, a social revolution was taking place in the countryside. Relations between landlords and their tenants, always difficult, worsened in the late nineteenth century as Parnell (himself a Protestant landowner) used the land question as the locomotive to pull the Home Rule train. The government eventually decided to fund the buying out of the landowners by the sitting tenants, with the eventual result that Ireland became a country owned by thousands of small farmers instead of a few proprietors. The big houses of the latter were left in most cases with only their demesnes. Most landlords, in debt and despair, welcomed land purchase and left the country. Their legacy, often neglected, sometimes deliberately destroyed, was the crumbling houses and demesne walls which still characterise rural Ireland. As a class, the Protestant ascendancy largely ceased to exist.

In 1916, while the First World War was going on, indeed going badly for Britain and her allies, the Easter Rising broke out in Dublin. This was the work of a small but determined band of revolutionaries for whom England's difficulty was Ireland's opportunity. Seizing the General Post Office in Sackville (now O'Connell) Street and other strong points, Patrick Pearse and his followers were dislodged only when artillery was used. By the time the rebels surrendered, the centre of Dublin looked like a battle-scarred town in Flanders. Most people disapproved of the rising, but opinion changed when the leaders were subsequently tried under martial law and shot. As the poet William Butler Yeats put it in his poem 'Easter 1916' - 'all changed, changed utterly.' In the 1918 elections the party of the republicans, Sinn Fein, swept aside the Home Rule party in most of the country. Its military wing, the Irish Republican Army, led by Michael Collins, then launched a guerrilla war against the forces of the crown and its supporters. The eventual outcome was the partition of the country and an Anglo-Irish treaty under which the majority in Sinn Fein and the IRA accepted a good deal less than the completely independent republic they had been seeking. The minority, led by Eamon De Valera, repudiated the treaty and a short but brutal civil war followed between the Free Staters and the Republicans. The pro-treaty party won and proceeded to establish the Irish Free State. In the north, six counties with Protestant majorities remained within the United Kingdom, under a provincial government in Belfast.

Since 1922 the two parts of Ireland have developed differently. The Irish Free State, which started with dominion status within the British Empire, gradually mutated into the Republic of Ireland (officially declared in 1949). Under De Valera, who after the civil war entered politics as leader of a new party, Fianna Fail, the Free State became increasingly Catholic in ethos and conservative in social outlook. The contrast with Northern Ireland, where Protestant Unionist governments feared the substantial Catholic and nationalist minority in their midst, was deepened by the Second World War, in which the south stayed neutral while the north played a vital part as a base for anti-submarine operations in the North Atlantic and as a training ground for American troops on the way to Normandy. It should be pointed out, however, that more southerners than northerners enlisted in the British forces and that fire brigades from the south helped to douse the flames in Belfast after the Blitz in 1941. Every election in the north was fought on the basic issue of pro- or anti-Partition, with occasional outbreaks of violence from the remnants of the IRA to keep Unionist nerves on edge and Protestant prejudices intact.

The 1960s, the immediate background to the most recent troubles, seemed to promise better things. The then taoiseach, Sean Lemass, created history by visiting Belfast at the invitation of a more liberal Unionist prime minister, Terence O'Neill. Catholic hopes and demands for equal civil rights rose; so too, unfortunately, did traditional Protestant fears. The civil rights campaign, which had broad support, soon succeeded in achieving its main demands, but not before extremists on both sides had been roused to arms. Following a split in the republican movement a revived IRA, better funded and armed than ever before, embarked upon a guerrilla war and terrorist campaign lasting twenty-five years. In that time, more than 3,000 people were killed, thousands more injured, many lives blighted, many livelihoods ruined and million of pounds worth of property destroyed. Yet, as a former public servant of impeccably nationalist credentials has recently put it: 'There was ... in all that time, or in the earlier period, no injustice, no unfairness, no degree of discrimination that was worth the sacrifice of a single life' (Maurice Hayes, *Minority Verdict*, 1995, p.319). Equally, nothing could justify the sectarian murders carried out by extreme Protestant or loyalist groups during the same period.

When the paramilitary forces on both sides eventually called ceasefires in 1994, the people of the north enjoyed the almost-forgotten pleasures of peace so much that hopes of a negotiated settlement acceptable to all but extreme fanatics began to seem realisable. International factors, especially American influence, had played an important part in creating this opportunity for a new start. President Clinton's visit to Belfast in November 1995 was the climax of this hopeful mood. Unfortunately, the optimism he expressed so eloquently was subsequently blunted, when the IRA refused to declare its ceasefire permanent or to disarm in any way before a final political settlement acceptable to its members had been negotiated. Without some such reassurance that terrorism was over for good, neither the British nor the Irish governments, let alone the Unionist parties, would enter into negotiations with the republican movement's political wing, Sinn Fein. Worse still, early in 1996 the IRA resumed its campaign in Great Britain with enormously destructive bombs in London and Manchester. The Orange Order then put the police in an impossible position in July of the same year by insisting on its right to march along a traditional route at Portadown whose inhabitants, now largely Catholics, would not agree. The police chief, having initially banned the march, permitted it to proceed, after several days of serious rioting by Protestants. This capitulation in turn caused mayhem by disillusioned Catholics. So far, the ceasefire proclaimed by the loyalist groups has held, but at the time of writing, the prospects for a lasting peace are once more dark and uncertain.

Dr W.A. Maguire
Head of Human History
and acting Deputy Director

Significant Dates in Irish History

1603	Defeat of Hugh O'Neill and his allies by English forces, followed by the Flight of the Earls (1607) and the Plantation of Ulster (1609).
1641	Outbreak of rebellion against English rule.
1649	Conquest of Ireland by Cromwell, followed by wholesale transfer of Catholic-owned land to his soldiers and supporters.
1660	Restoration of Charles II, followed by a land settlement favourable to the former Cromwellians.
1689	Land settlement reversed by James II's Irish parliament but reimposed and extended after his defeat at the Boyne (1690).
1697-1709	Penal laws enacted by the Protestant parliament in Dublin against Catholics and Dissenters.
1720s	Beginning of Scotch-Irish emigration to America.
1740-41	Serious famine in Ireland.
1759	Guinnesss brewery established in Dublin.
1760s	Agrarian disturbances break out in Munster (Whiteboys) and Ulster (Oakboys and Steelboys) against rising rents and tithes.
1776	Declaration of American independence, followed by withdrawal of British troops from Ireland.
1778	The American privateer John Paul Jones captures HMS *Drake* in Belfast Lough. First Volunteer company formed in Belfast, the start of a national movement.
1780	Free trade for Irish merchants with British colonies conceded by the British government, after pressure from the Volunteers.
1782	Legislative independence for the Irish parliament conceded, after pressure from the Volunteers.
1789	Outbreak of the French Revolution.
1791	Formation of the first Societies of United Irishmen in Belfast and Dublin.
1793	Execution of Louis XVI. France declares war on England. Last of a series of Catholic relief acts gives Catholics the vote and removes other restrictions.
1795	Formation of the Orange Order, following fighting between Protestant Peep O'Day Boys and Catholic Defenders in County Armagh.
1796	French invasion fleet arrives off County Cork but fails to land.
1798	Outbreak of insurrection in Ireland, especially in Counties Wexford, Antrim, Down and Mayo. Defeat of the rebels followed by severe repression.
1800	Act of Union makes Ireland part of the United Kingdom.
1829	Catholic Emancipation is achieved following O'Connell's successful mass campaign.
1845-7	Great Famine, followed by mass emigration to America.
1870s and 1880s	Land agitation and rise of Charles Stewart Parnell as leader of the Home Rule movement, leading to Gladstone's Land Acts and first Home Rule Bill.
1886	Formation of Irish Unionist party. Defeat of Gladstone's Home Rule Bill.
1891	Fall of Parnell, followed by defeat of Gladstone's second Home Rule Bill.
1903	Wyndham's Land Purchase Act, the most sweeping of several by which tenants replaced landlords as owners of the soil.
1912	Third Home Rule Bill introduced. Unionists prepare to resist it by force.
1914	Home Rule Act passed but suspended following outbreak of war in Europe.
1916	Easter Rising in Dublin suppressed after heavy fighting. Leaders subsequently tried by martial law and shot.
	Battle of the Somme, with heavy casualties amongst Irish regiments in France.

1919-21	Anglo-Irish War or Troubles, ending with a treaty establishing an Irish Free State in twenty-six of the thirty-two counties. Six Ulster counties opt to remain in United Kingdom.
1922-3	Civil War between Free State government and Republicans who refused to accept the Treaty. Victory of the Free Staters.
1937	De Valera issues a new constitution, abolishing dominion status and claiming jurisdiction over the whole of Ireland.
1939-45	Second World War. Eire neutral. Belfast Blitz of 1941. Northern Ireland important to the Allies for its ports, airfields and safe training facilities for D-Day armies (including many Americans).
1949	Republic of Ireland declared.
1960s	Rising hopes of Catholics in Northern Ireland. Sean Lemass, Dublin premier, visits Terence O'Neill in Belfast.
1968	Start of civil rights campaign.
1969-94	Guerrilla and terrorist campaign by IRA and Loyalist paramilitaries, ending with ceasefire.
1995	President Clinton visits Ireland and comes to Belfast.
1996	IRA ends its ceasefire with bombs in London and Manchester.
	Orange march at Portadown leads to serious disorder.

SELECTED BIBLIOGRAPHY

Bruce Arnold, *A Concise History of Irish Art* (London, 1977).

Wendy Baron, *Sickert* (London, 1973).

__________, *The Camden Town Group* (London, 1979).

J.C. Beckett, *The Making of Modern Ireland 1609-1923* (London, 1966).

Terence Brown, *Ireland: A Social and Cultural History 1922-79* (London,1981).

Julian Campbell, *The Irish Impressionists: Irish Artists in France and Belgium, 1850-1914*, exhibition catalogue, National Gallery of Ireland, 1984.

Anne Crookshank and The Knight of Glin, *The Painters of Ireland c.1660-1920* (London, 1978).

L.M. Cullen, *An Economic History of Ireland since 1660* (London, 1972).

Dennis Farr, *English Art 1870-1940* (Oxford, 1978).

R.F. Foster (ed.), *The Oxford Illustrated History of Ireland* (Oxford, 1989).

S.B. Kennedy, *Irish Art and Modernism 1880-1950* (Belfast, 1991).

__________, *Paul Henry* (Dublin, 1991).

Richard Killeen, *A Short History of Ireland* (Dublin, 1994).

Kenneth McConkey, *British Impressionism* (Oxford, 1989).

Herbert Read (ed.), *Unit 1: The Modern Movement in English Architecture, Painting and Sculpture* (London, 1934).

Richard Shone, *The Century of Change: British Painting Since 1900* (Oxford,1977).

Hugh B. Staples, *The Ireland of Sir Jonah Barrington: selections from his Personal Sketches* (Seattle, 1967).

A.T.Q. Stewart, *The Narrow Ground: Aspects of Ulster 1609-1969* (London,1977).

W. G. Strickland, *A Dictionary of Irish Artists* (Dublin and London, 1913).

Ellis Waterhouse, *Painting in Britain 1530-1790* (Melbourne, London, Baltimore, 1953).

Christopher Wood, *Victorian Painters* (Woodbridge, Suffolk, 1995).

Catalogue of Paintings

Unknown artist

1. Captain William Jackson (died 1688)
(late 1660s)

Inscr: 'William Jackson Esq. of Jackson Hall
Coleraine. A.D. 1667. Married Susanna daughter
of Sir Tristram Beresford Bart' t.l.
Oil on canvas 120.2 x 99.5 cm.
Purchased 1977.

Though the portrait dates from the late 1660s, the inscription and coat of arms were probably added after 1680, when Jackson built his family seat of Jackson Hall. An English settler and a resourceful and energetic character, Jackson became tenant of the Clothworkers' Estate, a large tract of land west of the river Bann, in 1663 and subsequently developed the village of Killowen, near Coleraine, County Derry. He died on 24 July 1688 and was buried at Coleraine.

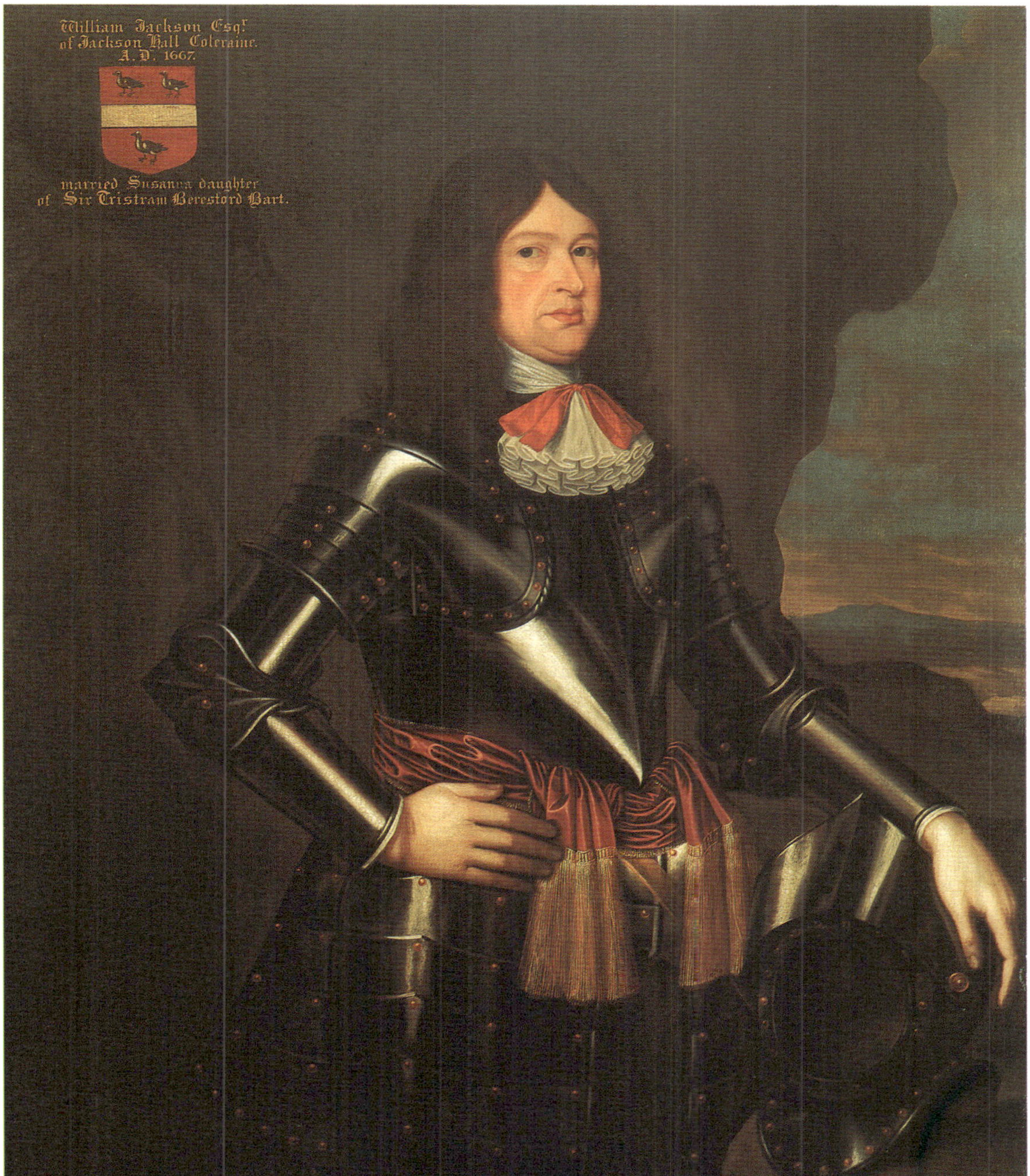
William Jackson Esqr.
of Jackson Hall Coleraine.
A.D. 1667.
married Susanna daughter
of Sir Tristram Beresford Bart.

Thomas Bate
(Irish, worked c. 1690)

2. Thomas, Lord Coningsby (1656-1729), Seated In A Romanticised Landscape, With A View Of The North Prospect Of Hampton Court, Herefordshire In The Background (1692)

Inscr: 'T. Bate fecit '92' b.l.
Oil on canvas 78.8 x 88.9 cm, oval,
contemporary frame.
Purchased London, 1973, with the aid of a grant
from the Friends of the National Collections
of Ireland.

Provenance: Painted for Thomas, Lord Coningsby; collection the Earl of Essex; collection Richard Arkwright; Burrell collection; collection Viscount Hereford; Christopher Gibbs; thereafter to Ulster Museum.

Bate is said to have been famous for his portraits painted on glass and to have lived mostly in Ireland; however, this is his only known signed work. The portrait shows Thomas, Lord Coningsby with his family seat in Herefordshire in the background. An ardent supporter of William III, Coningsby served the king in Ireland 1690-92 and was eventually elevated to the English peerage. He wears a colourful version of Roman military dress, popular in seventeenth century portraiture.

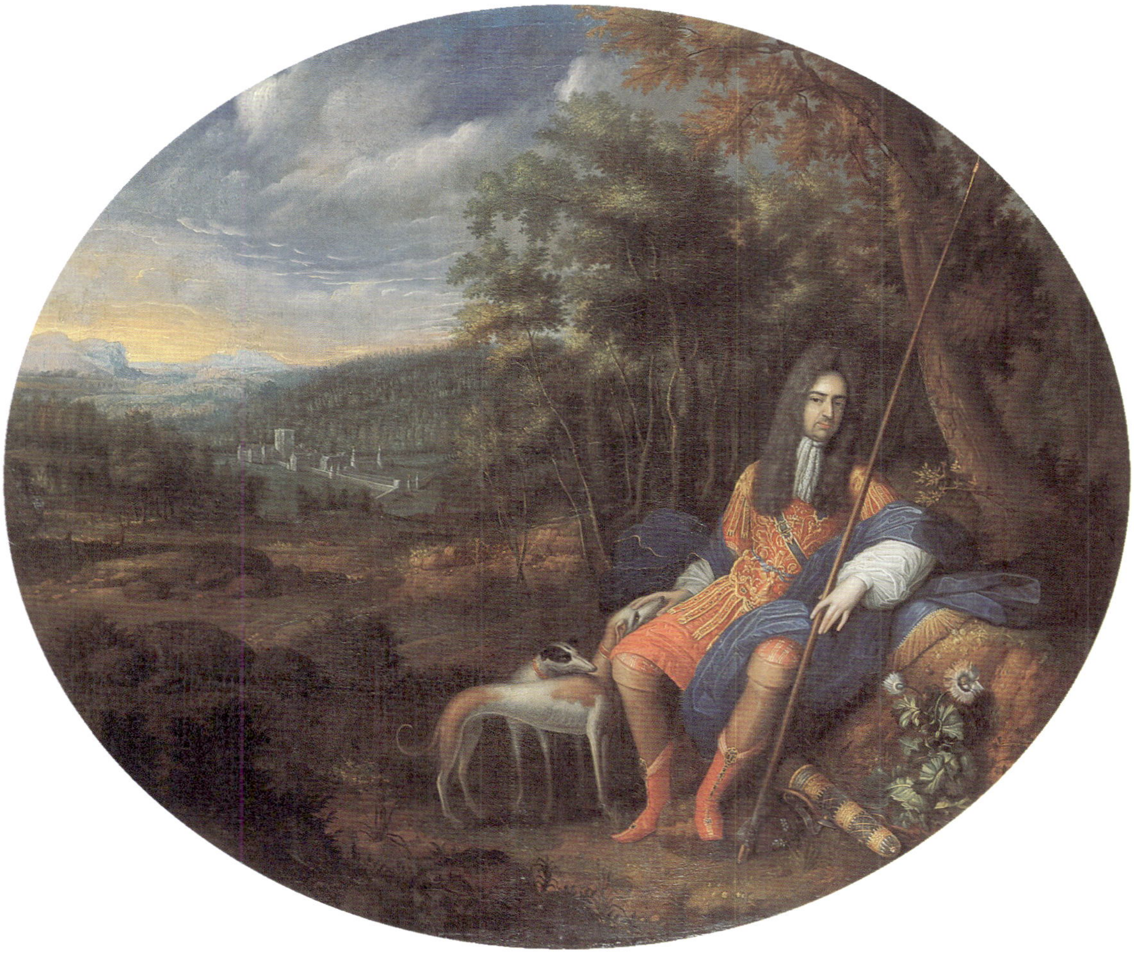

James Latham
(Irish, 1696-1747)

3. Captain Charles Janvre De La Bouchetière (died c. 1743) (1730-35)

Not inscribed.
Oil on canvas 126 x 97 cm.
Purchased 1978.

The most distinguished Irish portrait painter of the time, Latham studied in Antwerp and worked in Dublin from 1725. His sitters included prominent members of the establishment and Huguenot settlers such as the cavalry officer Captain de la Bouchetière. The portrait, with its delicate handling and overall sophistication, is amongst Latham's finest.

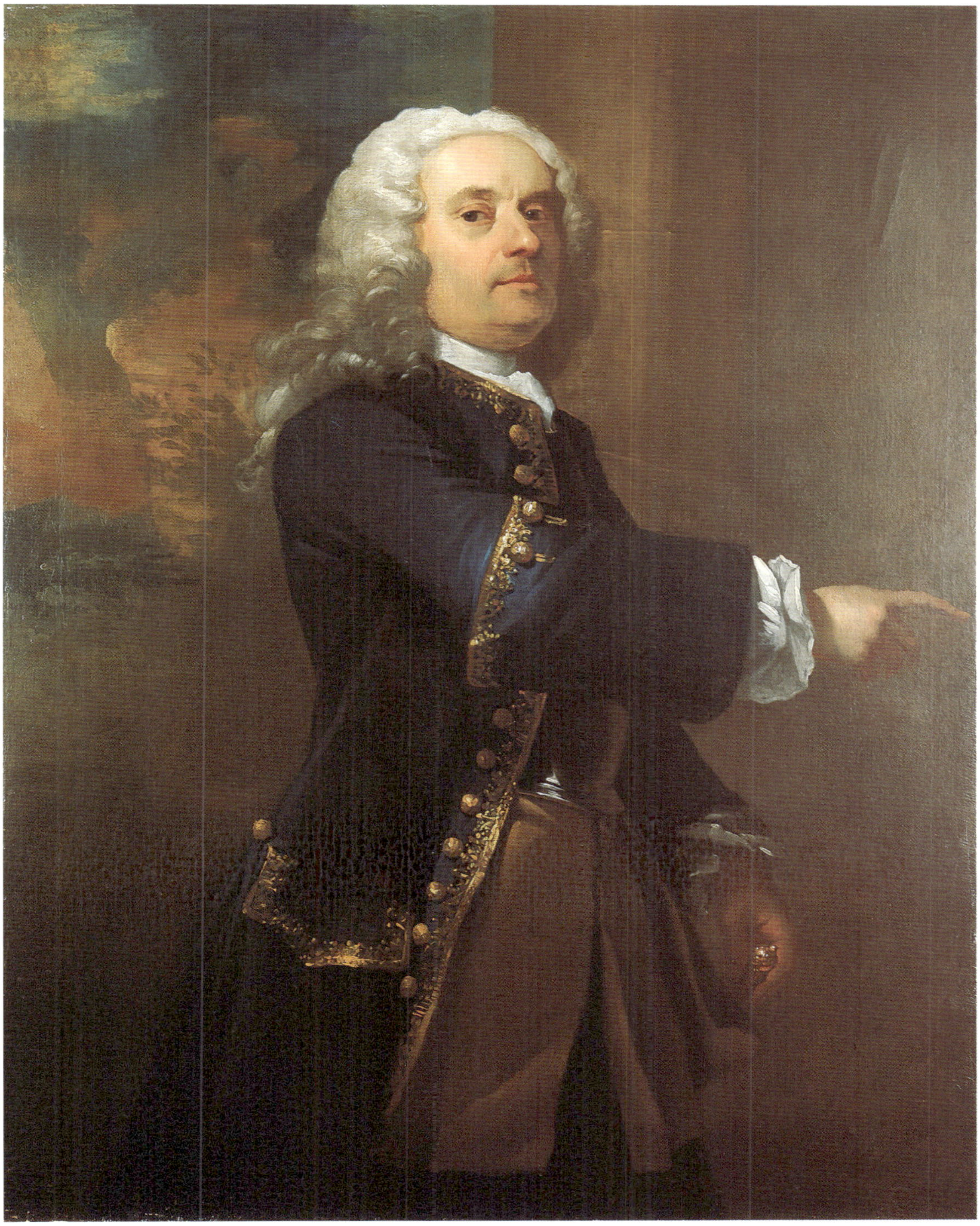

Richard Carver
(Irish, died 1754)

4. Landscape With Figures

Inscr: 'Rd. Carver' b.l.
Oil on canvas 101 x 131.5 cm.
Purchased 1968.

Carver, who was born in Waterford, pursued a successful career in Dublin as a painter of landscapes and historical subjects. *Landscape with Figures* is an interesting amalgam of Italian and northern influences; however, the tree in the centre, which effectively divides the picture in half, is artistically unsatisfactory.

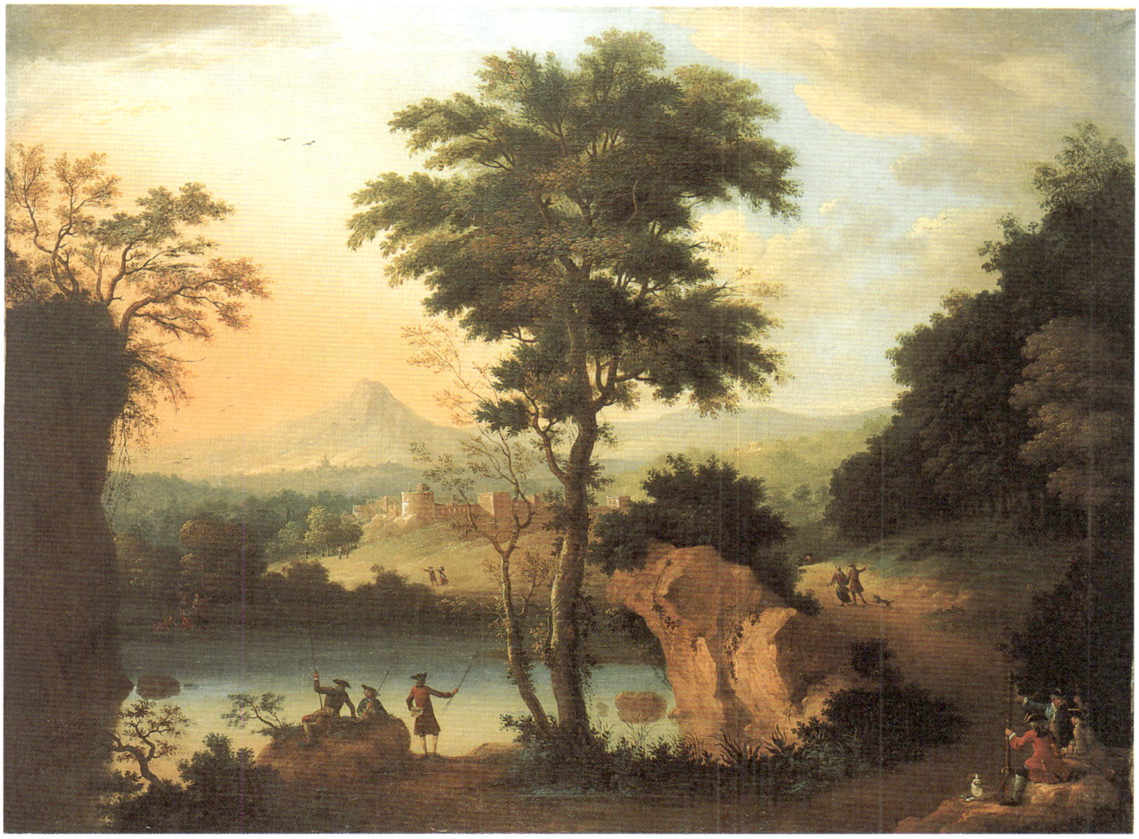

John Lewis
(Irish, worked 1740-69)

5. Portrait Of An Unknown Man
(1748)

Inscr: 'Jn. Lewis 1748' b.r.
Oil on canvas 74.8 x 25.8 cm.
Purchased 1989.

Probably of English origin, Lewis had a successful portrait practice in Dublin from 1740 and also worked as a scene painter in the city's Smock Alley theatre. Though many of Lewis's patrons were from the theatrical world, the sitter's attire suggests that he is perhaps a merchant or a Dissenter or Quaker.

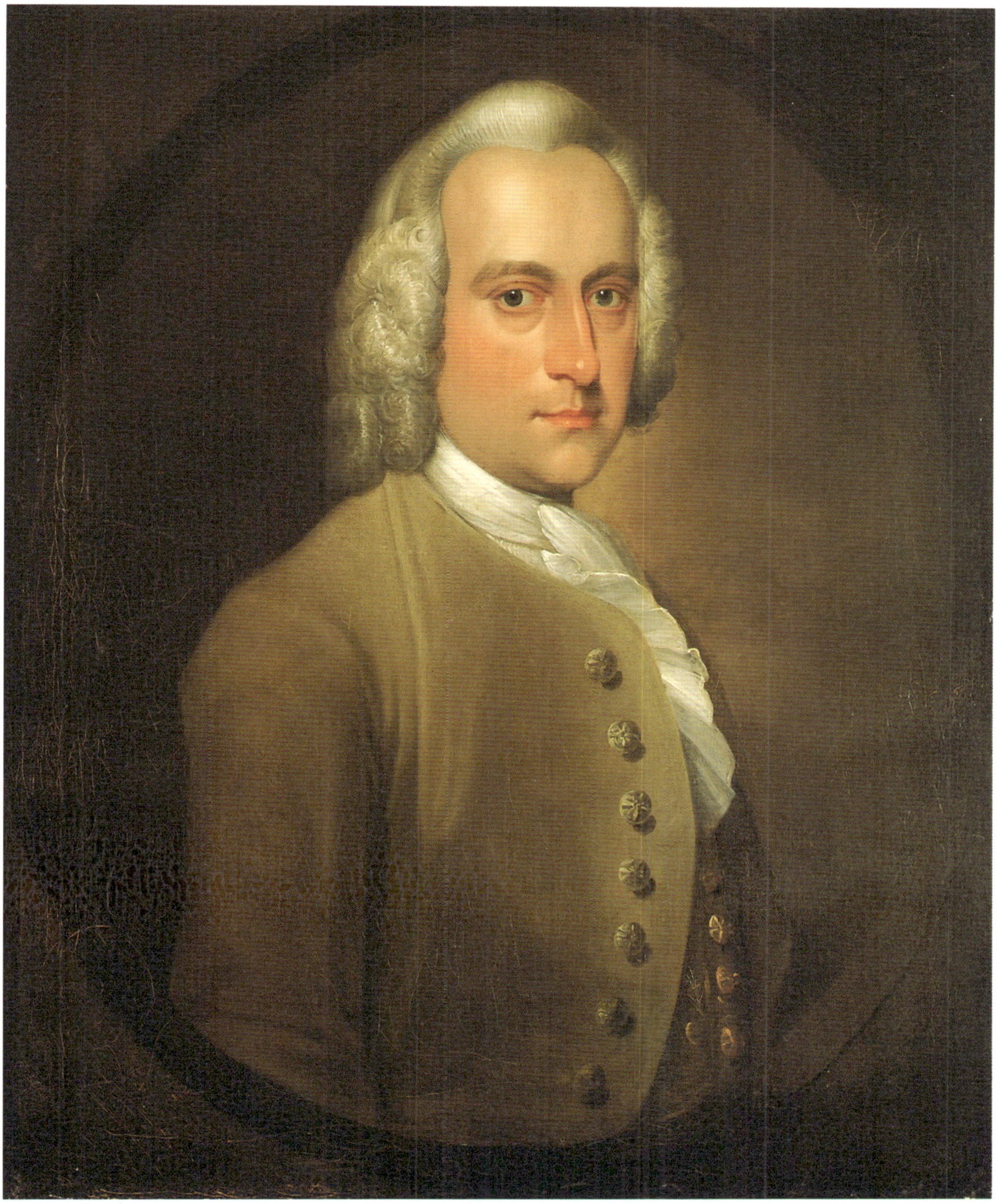

Thomas Mitchell
(British, 1735-90)

6. A View Of The River Boyne With Gentlemen And Horses By A Statue To William III In The Foreground, The Boyne Obelisk Beyond
(1757)

Inscr: 'T. Mitchell pinxit 1757' l.c.

Oil on canvas 106.8 x 175.5 cm.

Purchased 1990.

Provenance: The painting may have been commissioned by William Cavendish, 4th Duke of Devonshire and Lord Lieutenant of Ireland 1754-6, as a celebration of his connections with Ireland.

Mitchell, a shipbuilder and assistant surveyor to the Royal Navy, also worked as a marine artist and painted in Ireland in the late 1750s. This landscape, decidedly un-Irish in appearance, is partly imaginary. There is no evidence to suggest that there was ever a statue of William III on this particular site; Mitchell's aim in including the image was probably to glorify the Williamite victory of 1690. The obelisk commemorating the victory, shown in the background, was blown up by persons unknown in 1922.

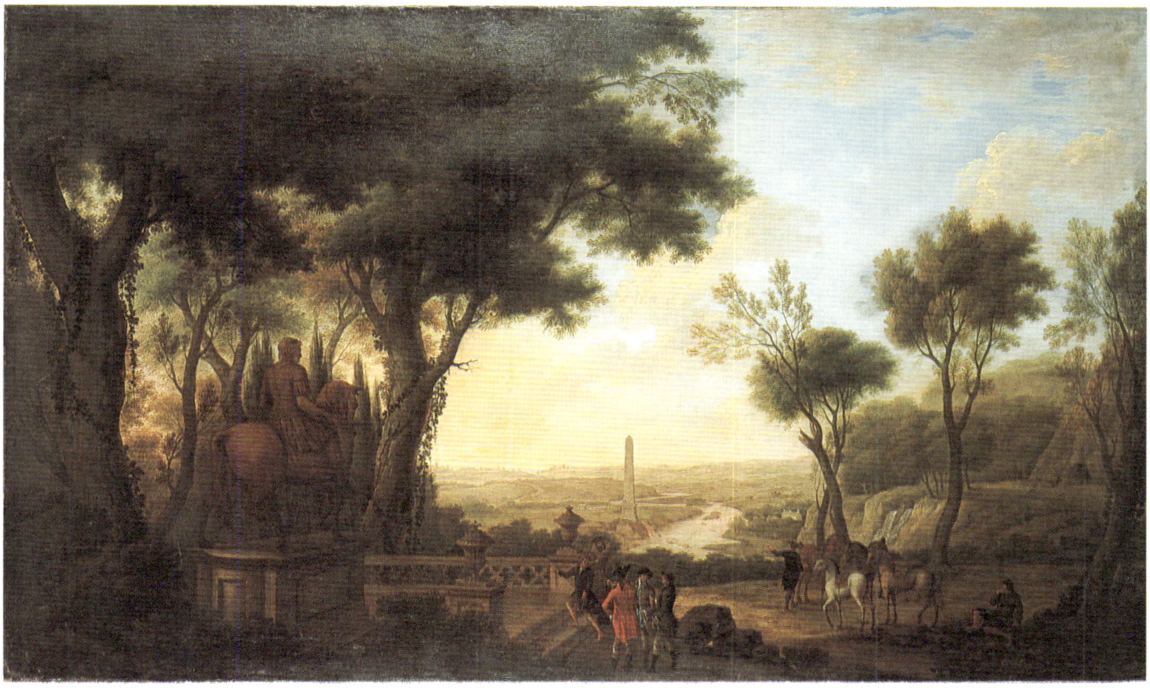

Nathaniel Hone
(Irish, 1718-84)

7. A Boy Deliberating On His Drawing
(c. 1766)

Not inscribed.
Oil on canvas 63.5 x 76 cm.
Purchased 1969.

A native of Dublin, Hone established himself in London as a portrait painter in the early 1740s and achieved great success, numbering members of the Royal family amongst his sitters. The young boy in this work is his son Camillus (1759-1836), who likewise became an artist. Hone disliked the contemporary fashion for the Italianate and based his style firmly on Dutch art; the inclusion of a landscape by the Dutch painter Jan van Goyen in the background is symbolic of this preference. Nevertheless, Hone occasionally used classical elements in his work, as exemplified by the statuette of Victory being drawn by Camillus. The portrait appears to acknowledge his debt to both Dutch and classical influences.

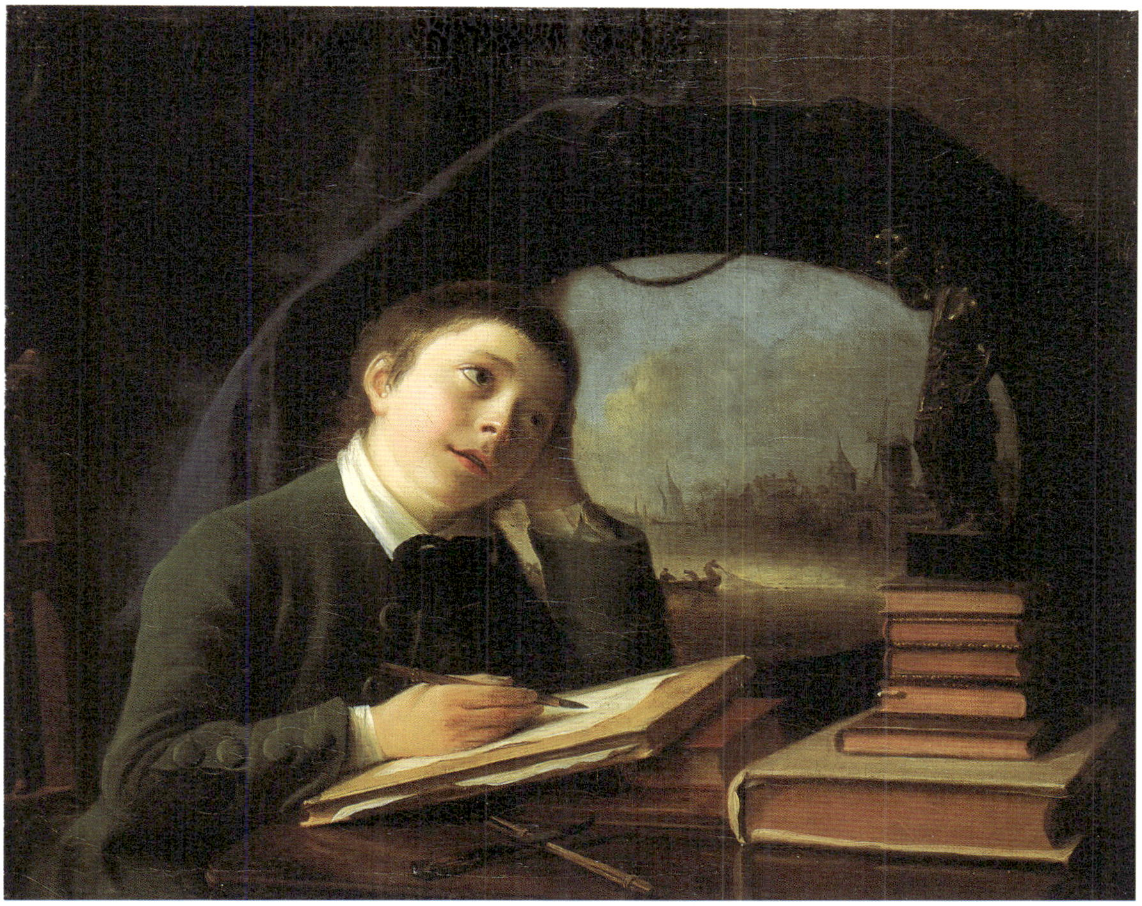

Sir Joshua Reynolds
(British, 1723-92)

8. Theodosia Magill, Afterwards Countess Of Clanwilliam (1743-1817)
(c. 1765)

Not inscribed.
Oil on canvas 127 x 101. 6 cm.
Purchased 1970, with the aid of grants from the National Art-Collections Fund, the Pilgrim Trust, the Gallaher-Mitchell Trust and local firms and individuals.

Provenance: Earls of Darnley to various owners; 1918, Leggatt Brothers, London to 1st Lord Brockett; 1937, 2nd Lord Brockett to Leggatt Brothers; 1939, bt. by C.F.C. Stout of New York; 1969, sold through Christie's to Leger Galleries, London; thence to Ulster Museum.

One of the most important figures in the history of British painting, Reynolds worked as a portraitist in London and Devon before a period of study in Italy 1749-52. Thereafter he became the leading portrait painter in Britain and was elected first president of the Royal Academy in 1768. Theodosia Magill, the daughter of Robert Hawkins Magill of Gill Hall, County Down, married Sir John Meade (created 1st Earl of Clanwilliam in 1776) in 1765.

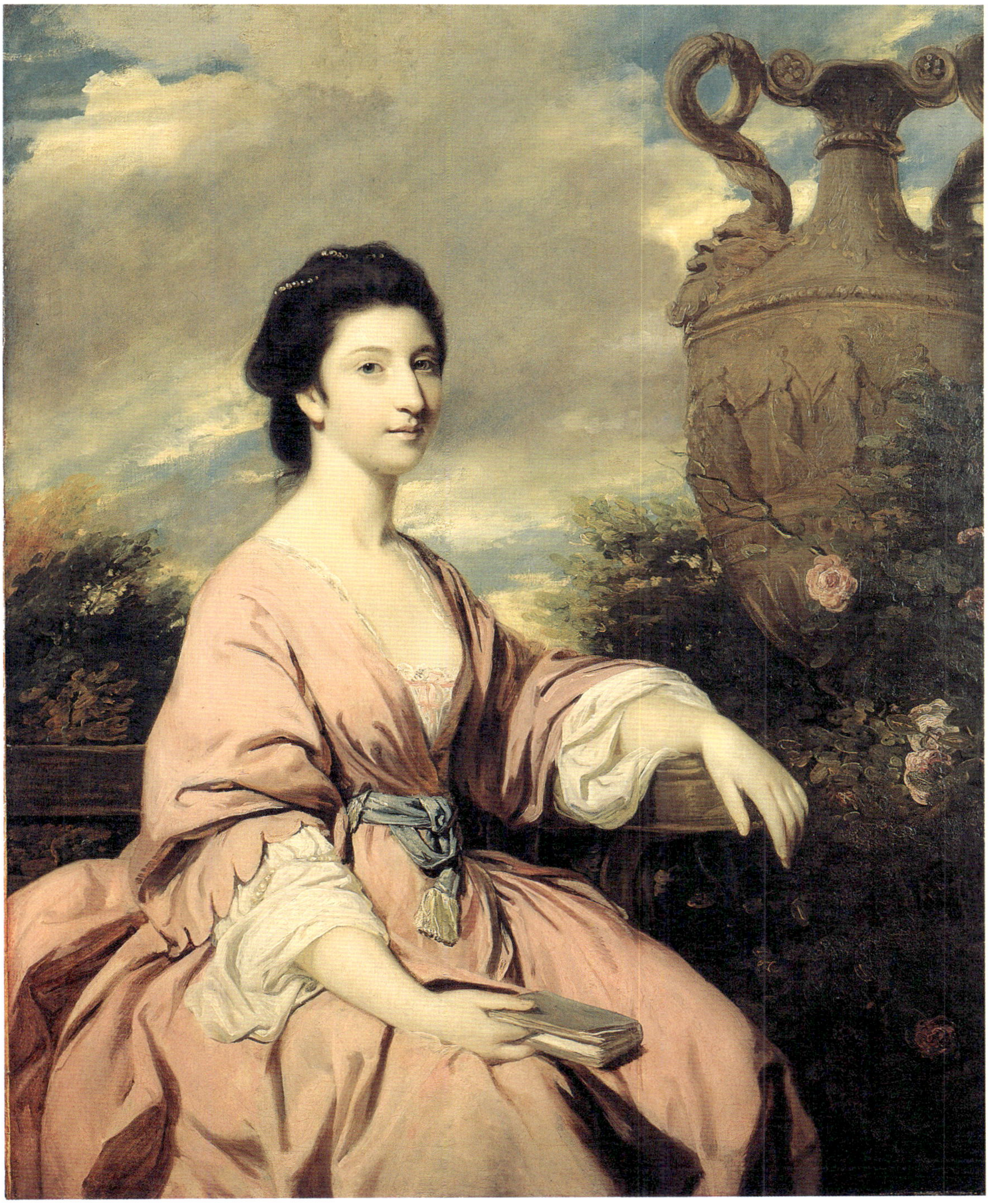

Jonathan Fisher
(Irish, died 1809)

9. View Of The Ferry And Castle Of Narrow Water
(c. 1771)

Not inscribed.

Oil on canvas 80.6 x 127 cm.

Purchased 1969.

Fisher exhibited regularly at the Society of Artists in Ireland 1765-80 and in 1795 published a volume of sixty engravings of scenery of various parts of Ireland after his own originals. The landscape shows Narrow Water Castle, County Down, built about 1560 and now in the care of the state, with the Newry river in the foreground. The engraving of the painting was published on 4 January 1772.

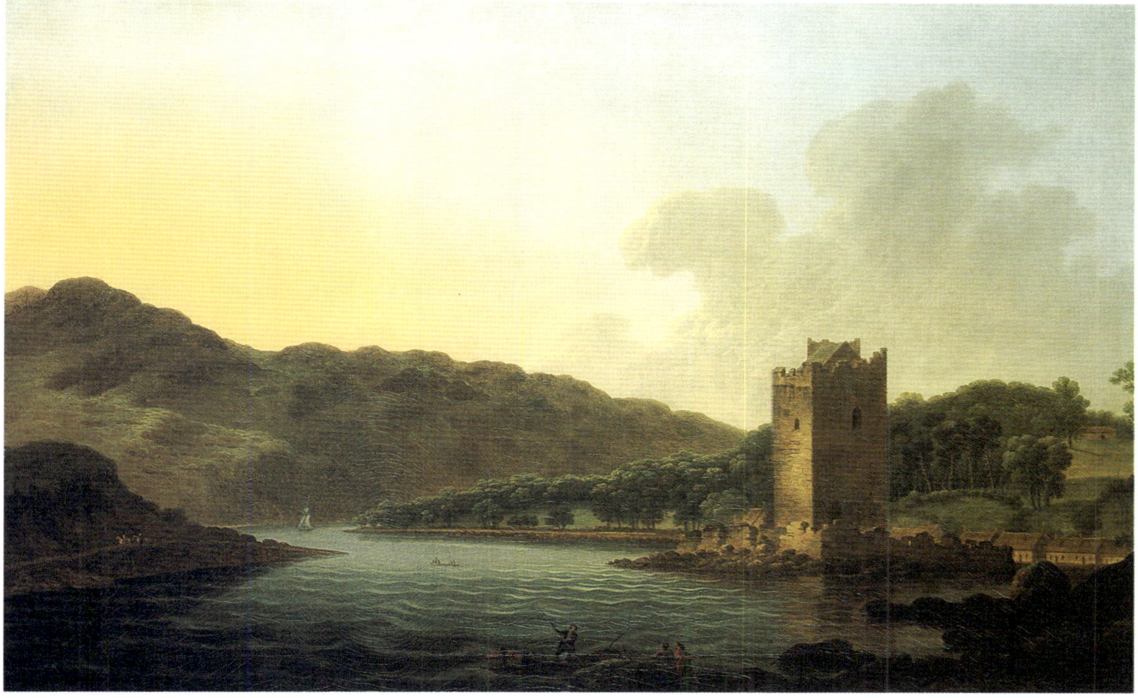

George Barret
(Irish, 1728 / 32-84)

10. The Waterfall At Powerscourt

Not inscribed.

Oil on canvas 73 x 70 cm.

Purchased 1964.

A student at the Dublin Society schools, Barret was influenced early in his career by the political writer and orator Edmund Burke, whose theories of the Sublime and Beautiful encouraged him to paint romantic scenery. The waterfall in the Powerscourt demesne in County Wicklow, a popular tourist attraction and a fitting example of the wild and overpowering forces of nature (the Sublime) was amongst his favourite subjects.

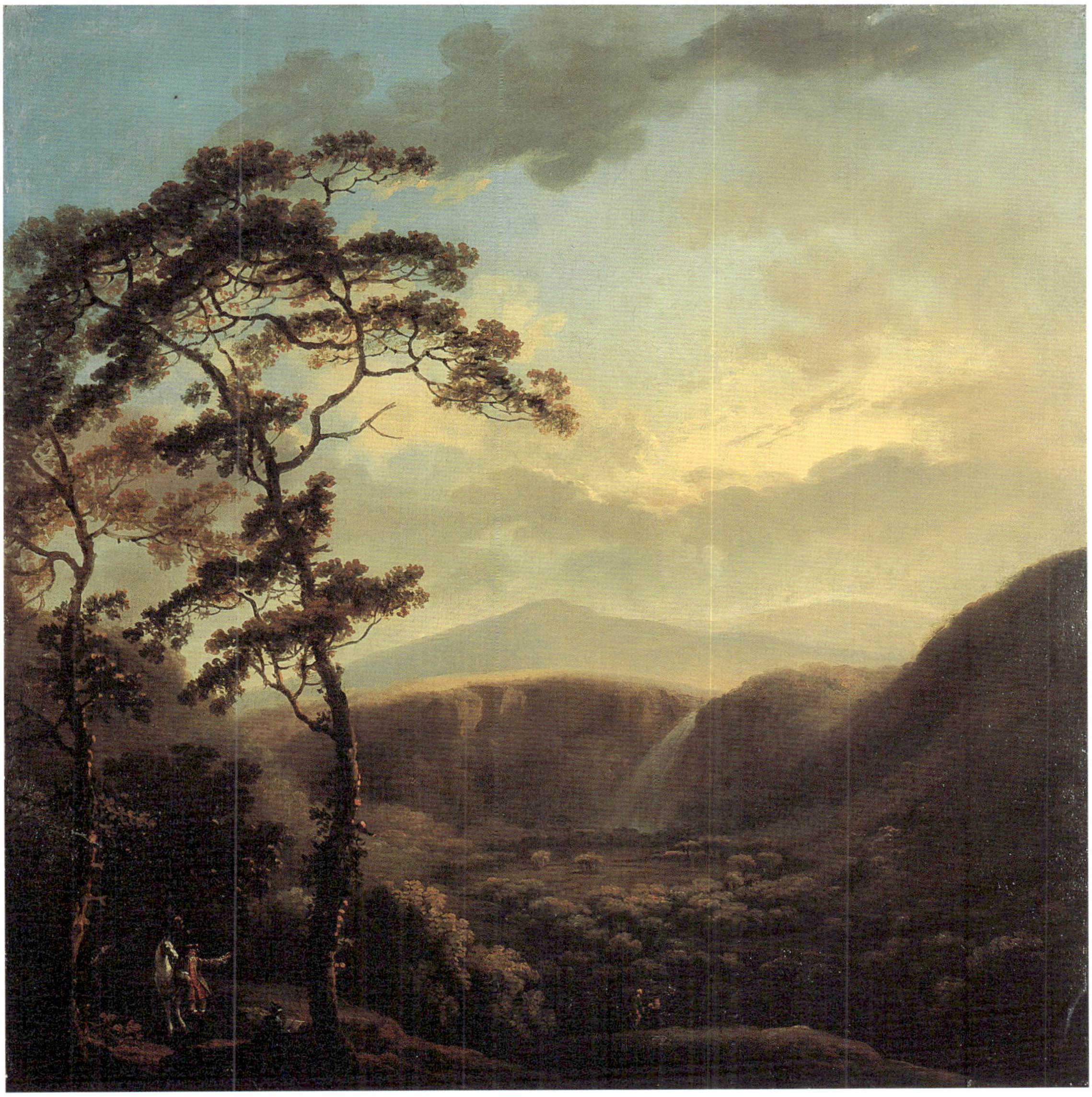

William Ashford
(English, worked in Ireland, 1746-1824)

11. Landscape With Carriage And Horses

Inscr: 'W. Ashford' on carriage.

Oil on canvas 72 x 89 cm.

Purchased 1975.

Provenance: Collection Lord Rockley, who purchased the picture from Leggatt Brothers, London in 1957. Sold by Lord Rockley in 1962; no further information.

Ashford, who came from Birmingham, settled in Ireland in 1764 and began exhibiting landscapes at the Society of Artists in Ireland in 1772. In 1823 he was elected first president of the Royal Hibernian Academy, a considerable honour for a landscape painter. The painting was originally thought to show Howth Castle, near Dublin; this, however, is incorrect and the location remains unknown. As with almost all of Ashford's work, the picture has a distinctly English air.

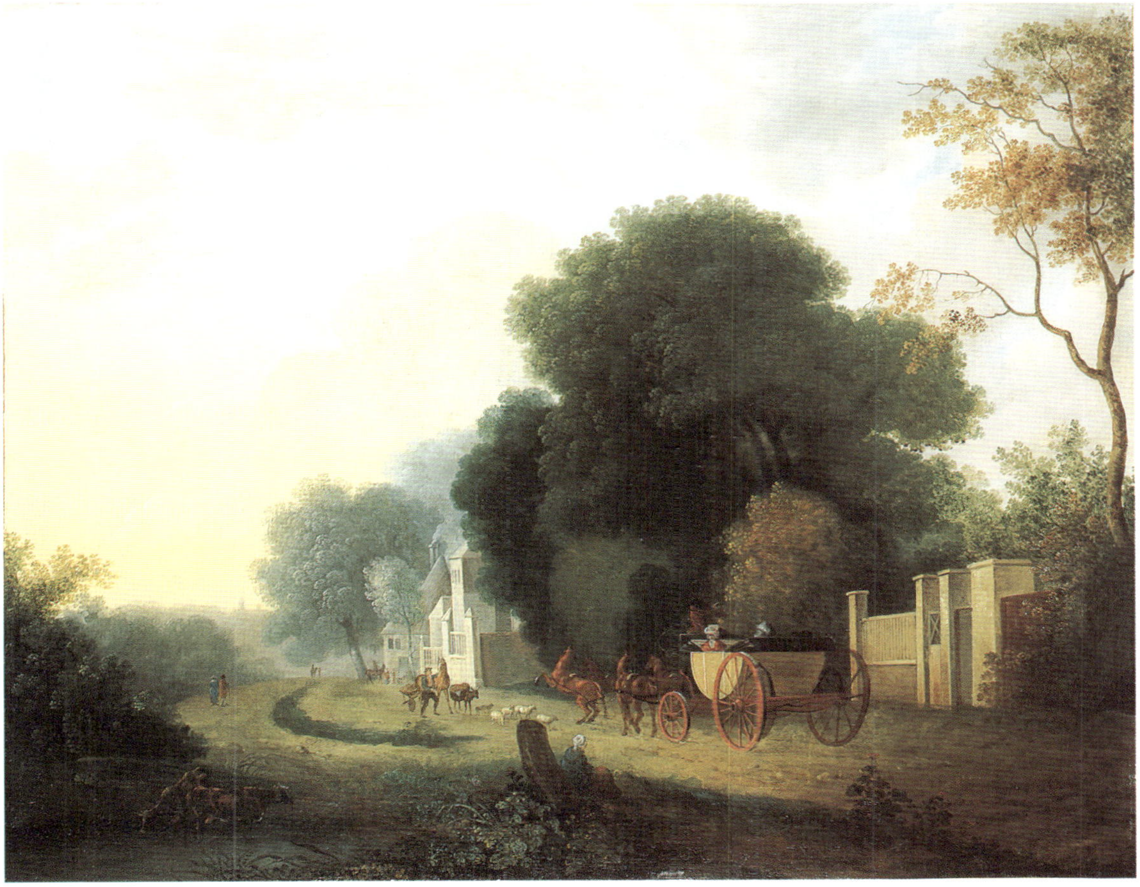

Strickland Lowry
(English, worked in Ireland, 1737-c. 1785)

12. Portrait Of A Lady
(c. 1780)

Not inscribed.
Oil on canvas 92.7 x 72.4 cm.
Purchased 1967.

The portrait and landscape painter Strickland Lowry, a native of Cumbria, moved to Belfast about 1762 and remained in Ireland until about 1780. This painting is a companion to a portrait, likewise by the artist, of a Lurgan Volunteer of 1780. The sitter nurses a little Bolognese dog, a form of toy poodle popular as a lap-dog in the eighteenth century.

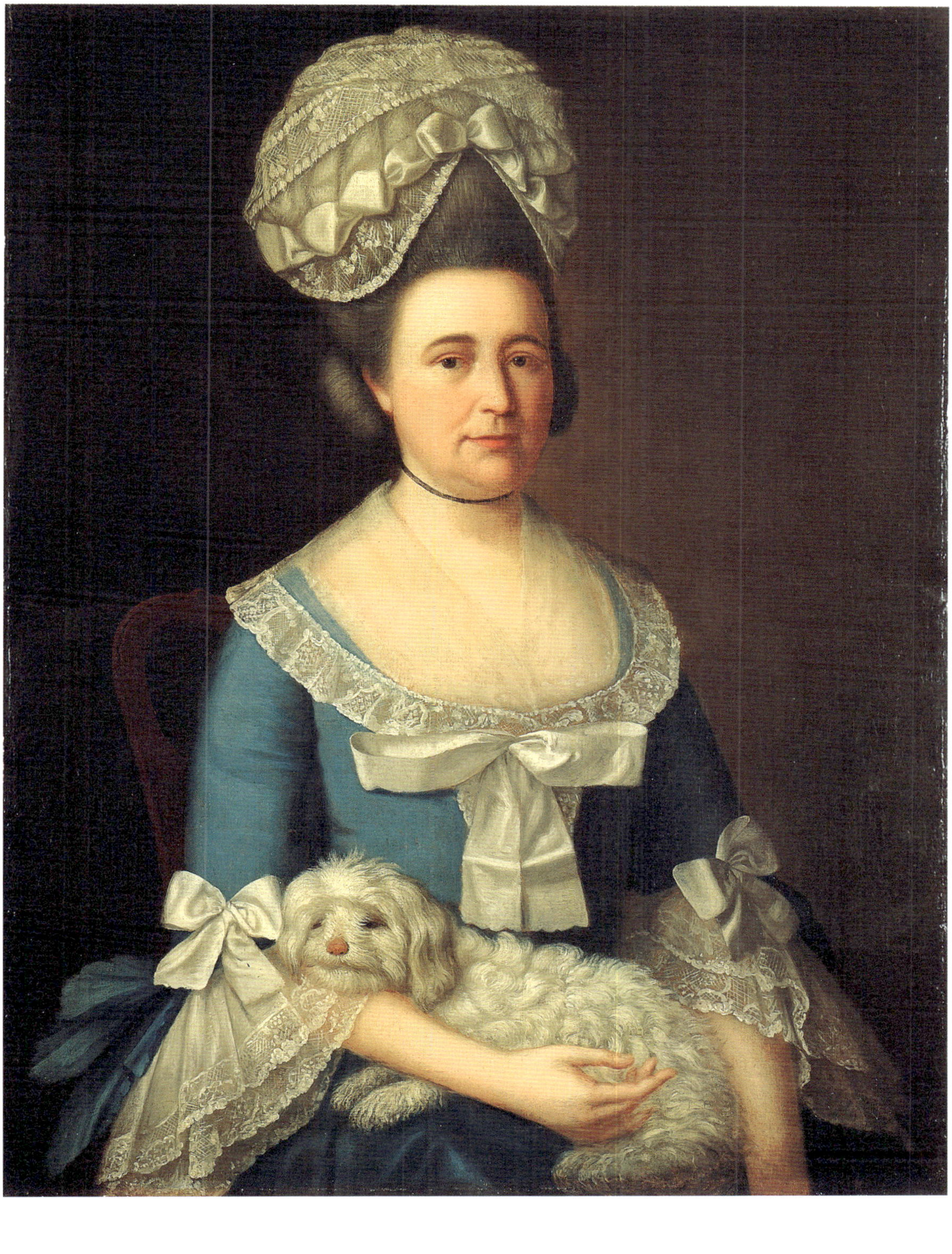

Joseph Wilson
(Irish, worked c. 1766-93)

13. Lieutenant Hugh Hyndman
(c. 1782)

Not inscribed.
Oil on canvas 77 x 64 cm.
Purchased 1974.

Wilson worked in Belfast and Dublin during the 1770s and 1780s and numbered amongst his sitters members of the Volunteer movement (a citizen army established in 1778 to defend Ireland against America and France during the American War of Independence, when British troops were withdrawn from Ireland to serve in America). The sitter, a lieutenant in the Belfast 3rd Volunteer Company, is almost certainly Hugh Hyndman, one of a family of prominent Belfast merchants.

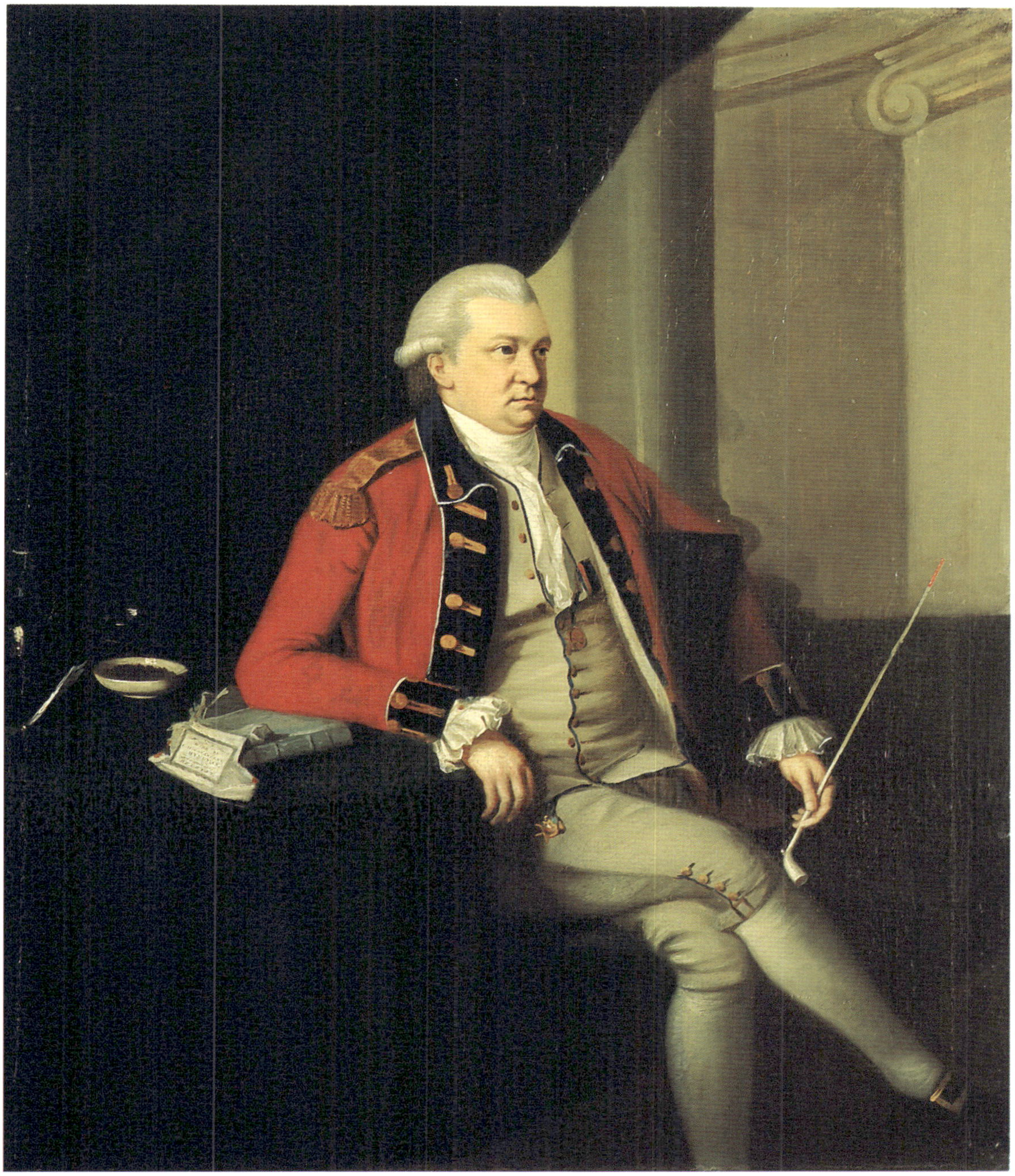

Hugh Douglas Hamilton
(Irish, 1740-1808)

14. JAMES MOORE O'DONNELL (1771-1806)
(c. 1795-6)

Not inscribed.
Oil on canvas 76.2 x 63.3 cm.
Donated by representatives of Sir Francis and Lady Stronge, per the Rt. Hon. Sir James H. Stronge, Tynan Abbey, County Armagh, 1925.
Provenance: By descent within the O'Donnell family.

One of the most important Irish portrait painters of the second half of the eighteenth century, Hamilton's sitters included members of the Royal family, nobility and persons making the Grand Tour (the latter painted during Hamilton's Italian sojourn 1779-92). The young man in this portrait was the second son of Sir Neal O'Donnell of Newport, County Mayo. A barrister and member of parliament, he was strongly opposed to the union of Great Britain and Ireland in 1800. He was killed in a duel on 14 September 1806.

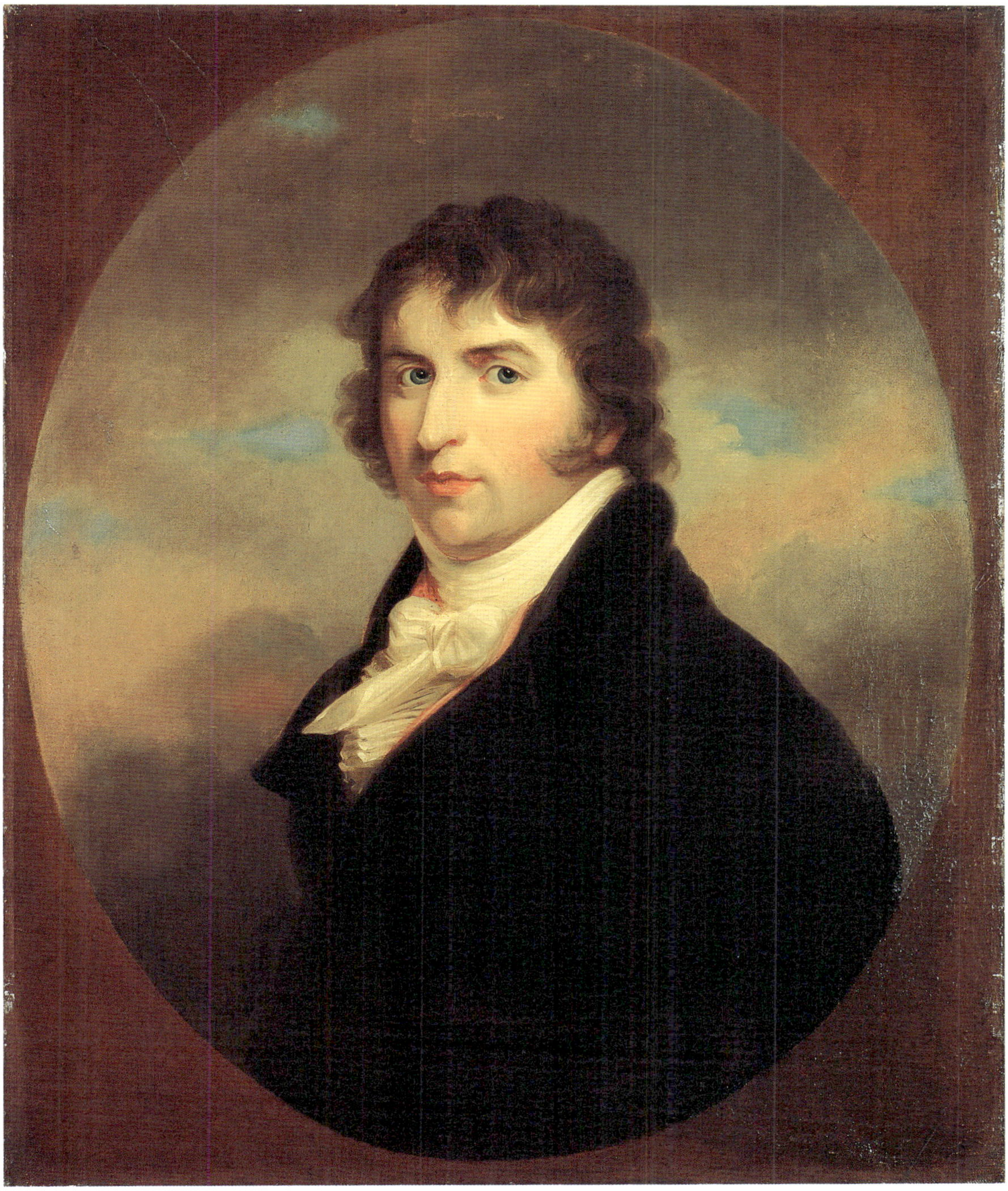

Joseph Wright (of Derby)
(British, 1734-97)

15. Virgil's Tomb: Sun Breaking Through A Cloud
(1785)

Inscr: '1785 JWP' b.r.

Oil on canvas 47 x 65 cm.

Purchased 1975.

Wright studied portrait painting in London under Thomas Hudson and was well established as a portraitist in Derby by the early 1760s. His candlelight scenes of contemporary scientific subjects, the result of his interest in the effects of light, brought him great renown. He probably painted six versions of *Virgil's Tomb*, of which this is the only known daylight scene. (The other images show the tomb by moonlight).

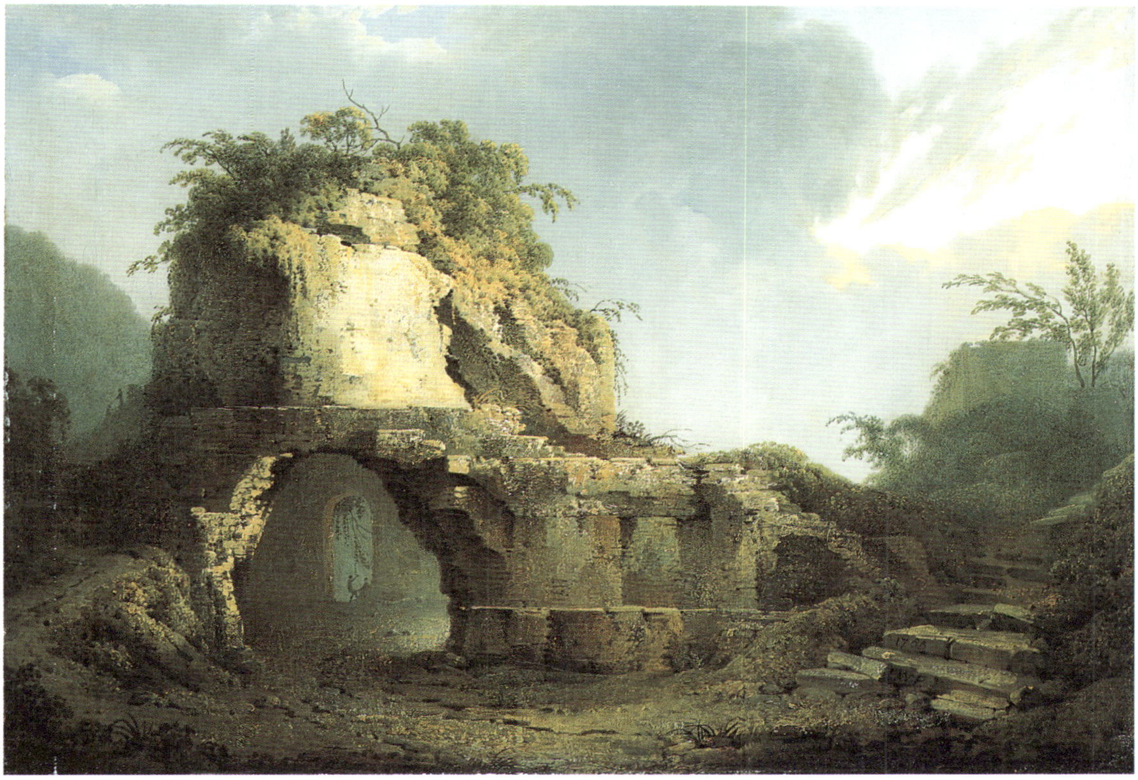

Sir William Beechey
(British, 1753-1839)

16. Portrait Of A Woman
(c. 1785-95)

Not inscribed.

Oil on canvas 75 x 62 cm.

Purchased 1970.

Portrait painter William Beechey studied at the Royal Academy schools and with Johann Zoffany and began exhibiting at the Academy in 1776. In 1793 he was appointed portrait painter to Queen Charlotte and subsequently received a knighthood. This portrait of an unknown elderly woman was probably painted in the mid-1790s, before Beechey took up society portraiture.

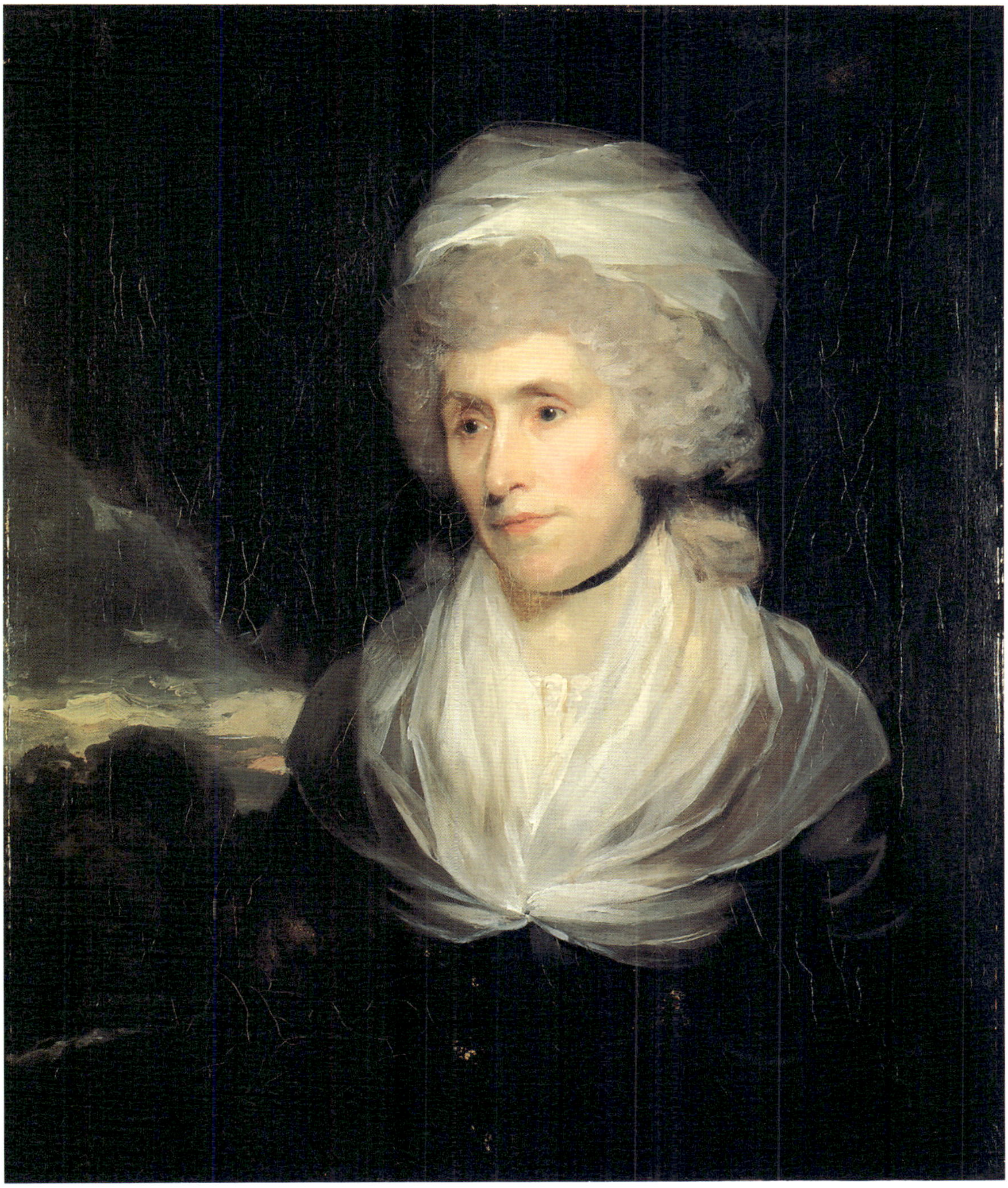

Francis Wheatley
(British, 1747-1801)

17. John O'Neill, 1st Viscount O'Neill of Shane's Castle (1740-98)
(c. 1780)

Not inscribed.
Oil on canvas 76.5 x 63.6 cm.
Purchased 1940.

Wheatley, a Londoner and painter of portraits and conversation pieces, moved to Dublin in 1779 to escape his creditors. He returned to his native city in 1783 and abandoned portraiture for genre subjects and scenes of sentimental realism, which brought him considerable acclaim. Viscount O'Neill, who sat to him during his Irish visit, died at Antrim in 1798 from wounds inflicted by a pikeman of the United Irish forces, in the rebellion by the United Irishmen in that year.

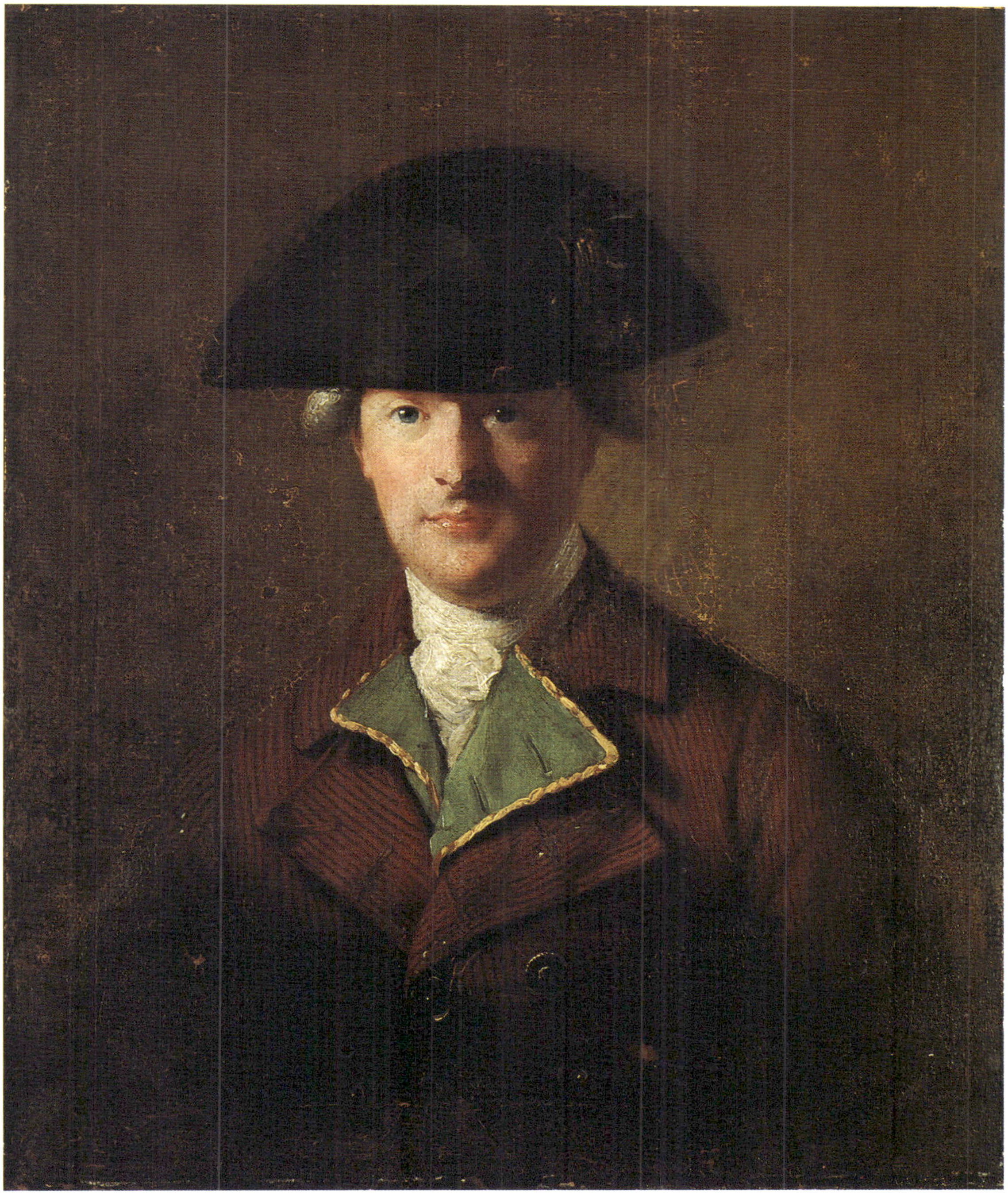

Thomas Robinson
(English, worked in Ireland, died 1810)

18. WILLIAM RITCHIE (1756-1834)
(c. 1802)

Not inscribed.
Oil on canvas 93.7 x 74.6 cm.
Donated by Alexander MacLaine, 1892.

A pupil of George Romney, Robinson settled in Ireland about 1790 and after three years in Dublin, moved north, firstly to Laurencetown, County Down and later to Lisburn, County Antrim. He thereafter lived in Belfast before finally returning to Dublin. William Ritchie, a close friend of the artist, founded the shipbuilding industry in Belfast in the early 1790s. The portrait shows Ritchie leaning against a statue of Neptune, with his shipyard prominent in the background.

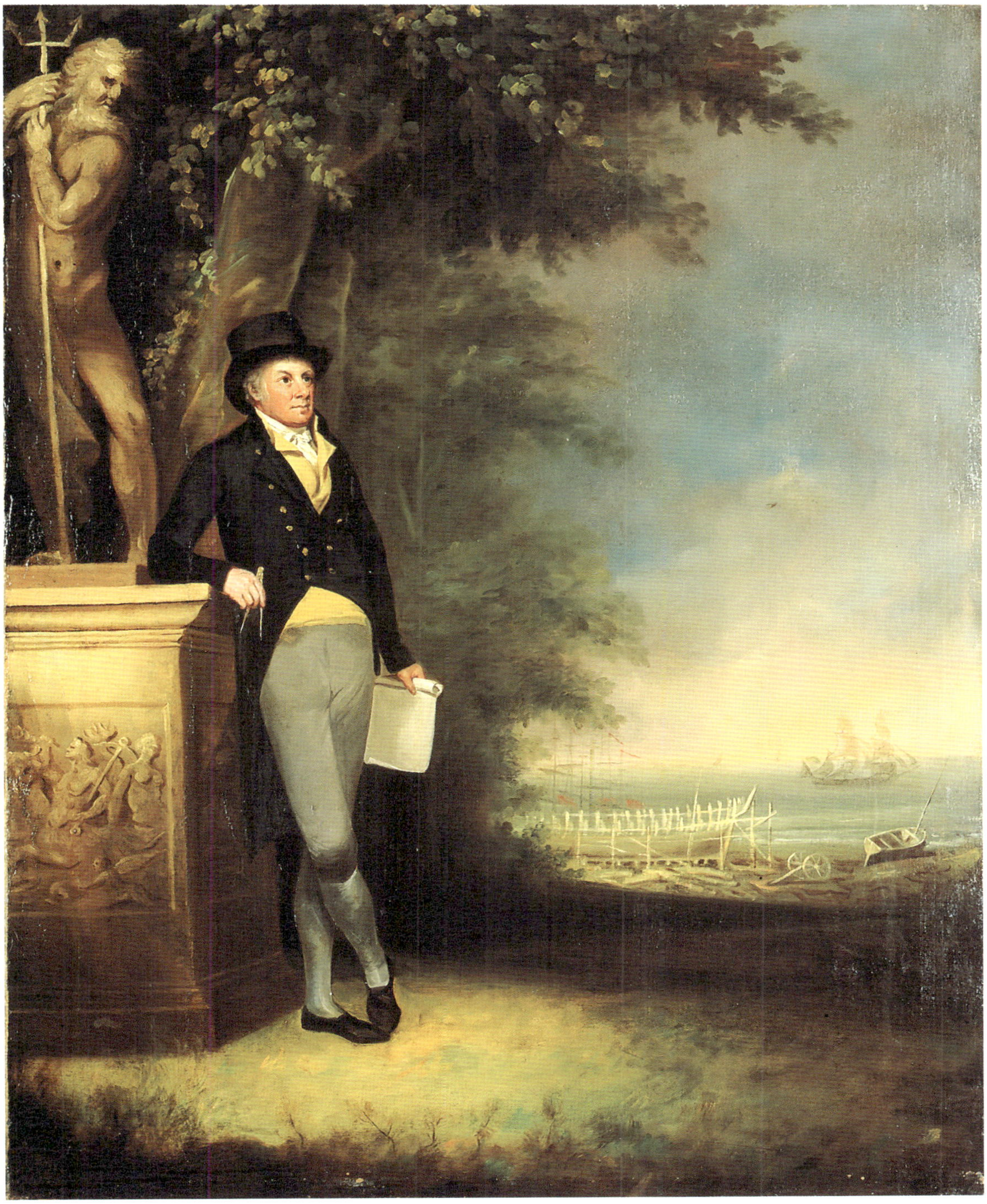

Joseph Peacock
(Irish, c. 1783-1837)

19. The Patron Or Festival Of St Kevin At The Seven Churches, Glendalough (1813)

Inscr: 'J. Peacock Pinxit 1813' l.

Oil on panel 86.4 x 137.8 cm.

Purchased 1964.

Provenance: Lord Deramore, Belvoir Park, Belfast, 1865; Lady Edith Dixon, Belfast, 1964; thence to Ulster Museum.

Peacock, a founder member of the Royal Hibernian Academy, exhibited regularly in Dublin 1809-35. This dramatic scene depicts the festival of St Kevin at Glendalough, County Wicklow, held annually on 3 June until suppressed by the Catholic church in 1862, on account of the drunkeness and general debauchery which accompanied the event. Peacock has ignored the devotional aspect of the day and has concentrated on the worldly celebrations of the occasion, such as drinking and dancing. The monastery at Glendalough, founded in the sixth century, was one of the most famous religious centres in early Christian Ireland.

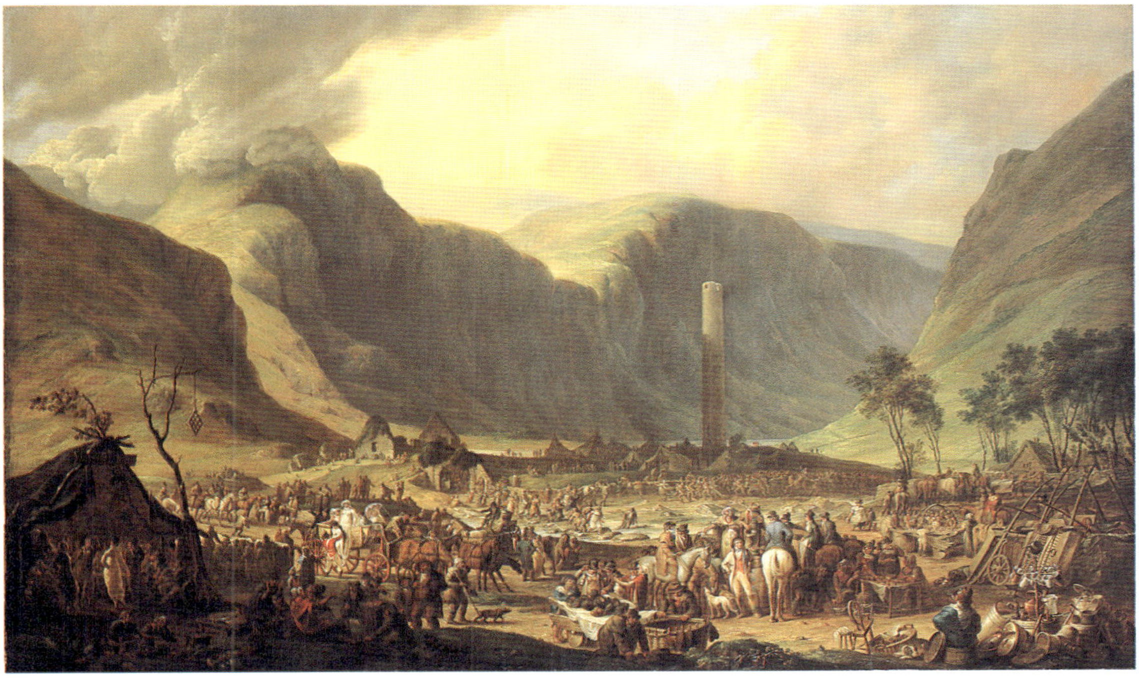

William Sadler II
(Irish, c. 1782-1839)

20. The Eagle's Nest, Killarney

Not inscribed.
Oil on panel 48.5 x 80 cm.
Purchased 1969.

Sadler was a regular exhibitor in Dublin and also taught painting, James Arthur O'Connor (following) being amongst his pupils. The Eagle's Nest, a conical-shaped mountain, is situated in the range of mountains at the Lakes of Killarney, an area which became popular with tourists in the mid-eighteenth century. The echoes around the Eagle's Nest were reputed to be the best in the Lakes. For this purpose, bugle-playing boatmen were available for hire by tourists; also, cannon were fired for special visitors on occasion. A cannon and bugler can be seen in the foreground.

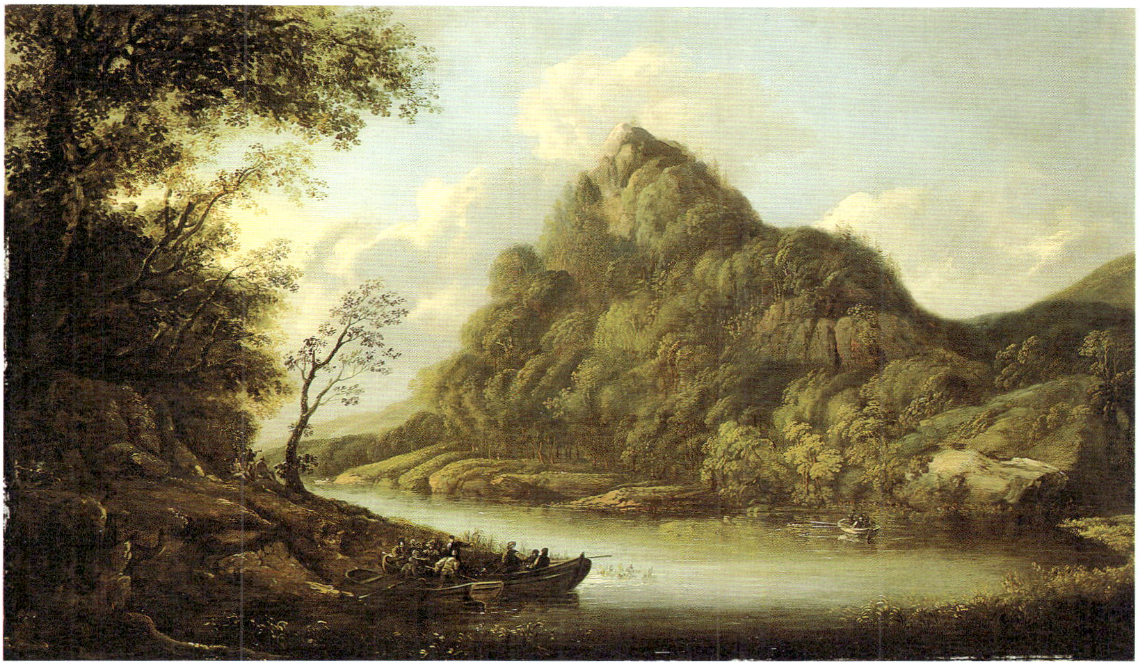

James Arthur O'Connor
(Irish, 1792-1841)

21. Scene In County Wicklow
(1820)

Inscr: 'J. A. O'Connor 1820' b.l.
Oil on canvas 70.8 x 91.3 cm.
Purchased 1970.

One of Ireland's best known landscapists, O'Connor settled in London in 1822 but continued to paint views of his native land. This scene, which could be set in some rustic Arcadia and not amongst the Wicklow Hills, was painted near Bray. The hills in the background are the Great Sugar Loaf and Little Sugar Loaf. The river meandering under the bridge is the Dargle.

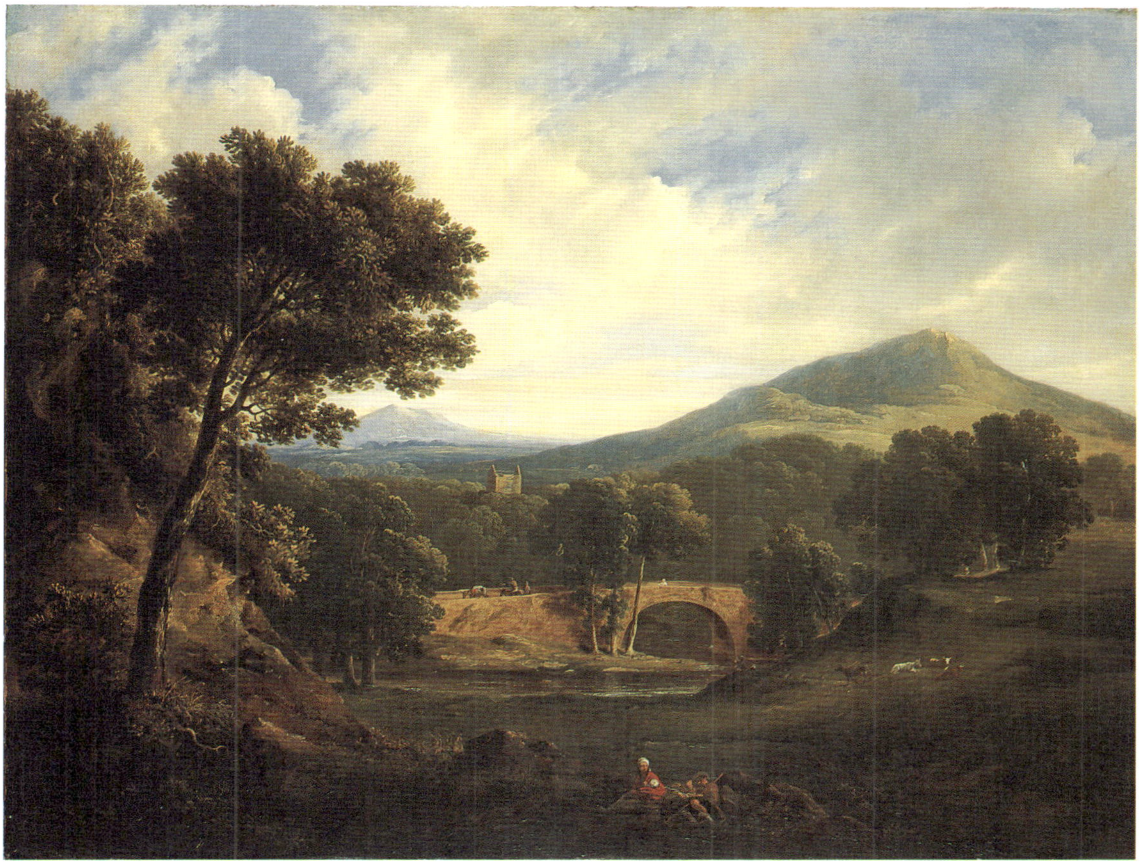

Martin Cregan
(Irish, 1788-1870)

22. Francis Johnston (1760-1829), His Wife And Two Nephews
(c. 1827)

Not inscribed.
Oil on canvas 97.7 x 80.3 cm.
Purchased 1971.
Provenance: By descent; R. Graves Johnston, the vendor, was a great-great grandson of Francis Johnston's brother Andrew.

Portrait painter Martin Cregan was born in County Meath and raised by foster-parents, whose name (Creggan) he took and later altered. After a period of study in Dublin and London, he settled in the former in 1822. This portrait shows Francis Johnston, his wife Anne and nephews Andrew and Robert (the smaller boy). Johnston is one of the greatest names in Irish architecture. Amongst his buildings in Dublin were the General Post Office and alterations to the Bank of Ireland (formerly Parliament House).

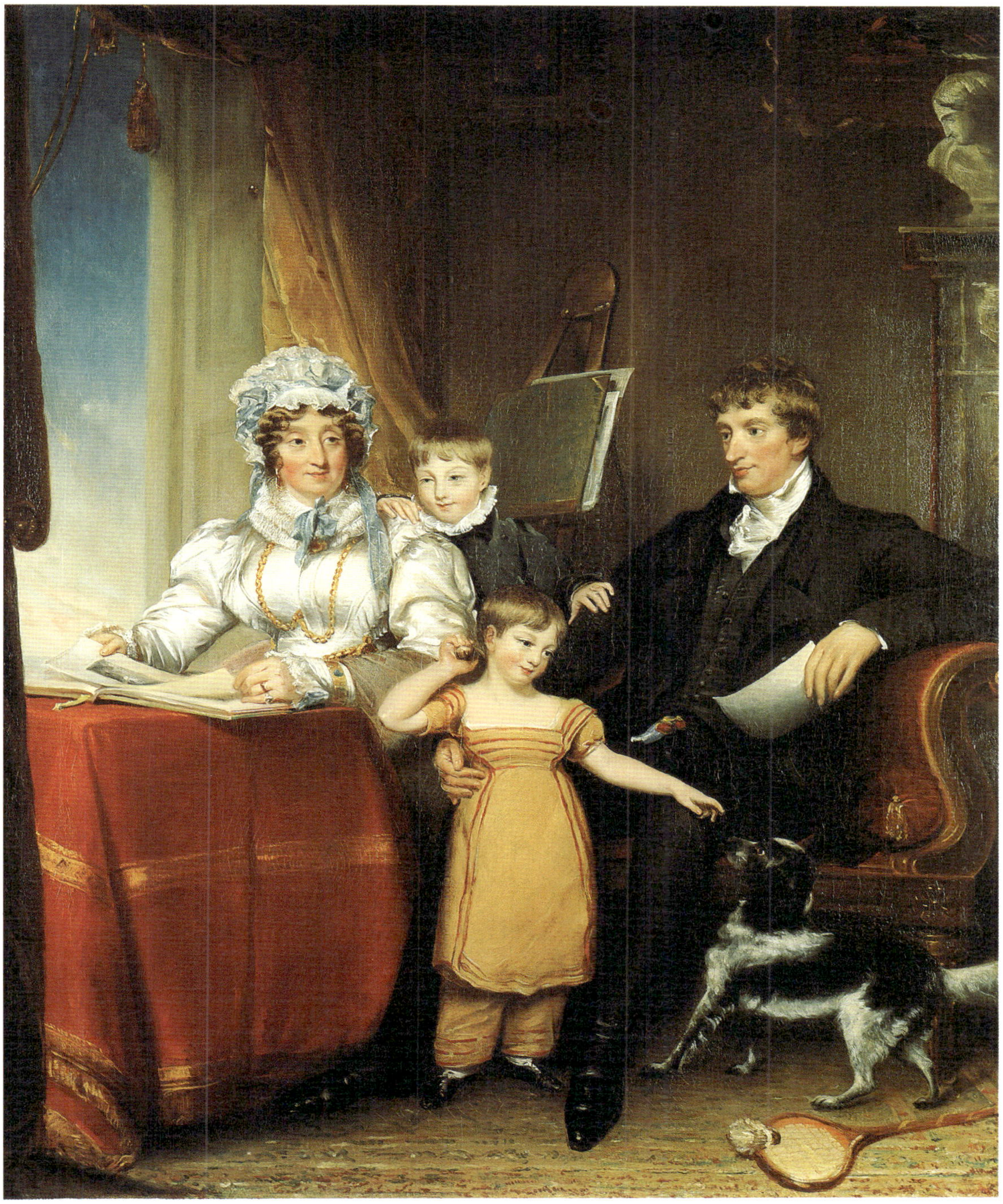

Joseph Paul
(British, 1804-87)

23. Mill Scene

Not inscribed.
Oil on canvas 122 x 91 cm.
Donated by Lady Edith Dixon, Belfast, 1959.

Joseph Paul of Norwich and London, a tantalisingly obscure figure, exhibited landscapes at the Norwich Society in 1823, 1829 and 1832. At some point thereafter, he got into trouble, was outlawed and not heard of for almost forty years. Eventually he was discovered running a studio in or near London, where he and his sons produced copies of the work of John Crome. This landscape, whilst not an exact copy of Crome, draws heavily on his work. Despite his questionable pursuits, however, Paul was a talented artist in his own right, as the painting testifies.

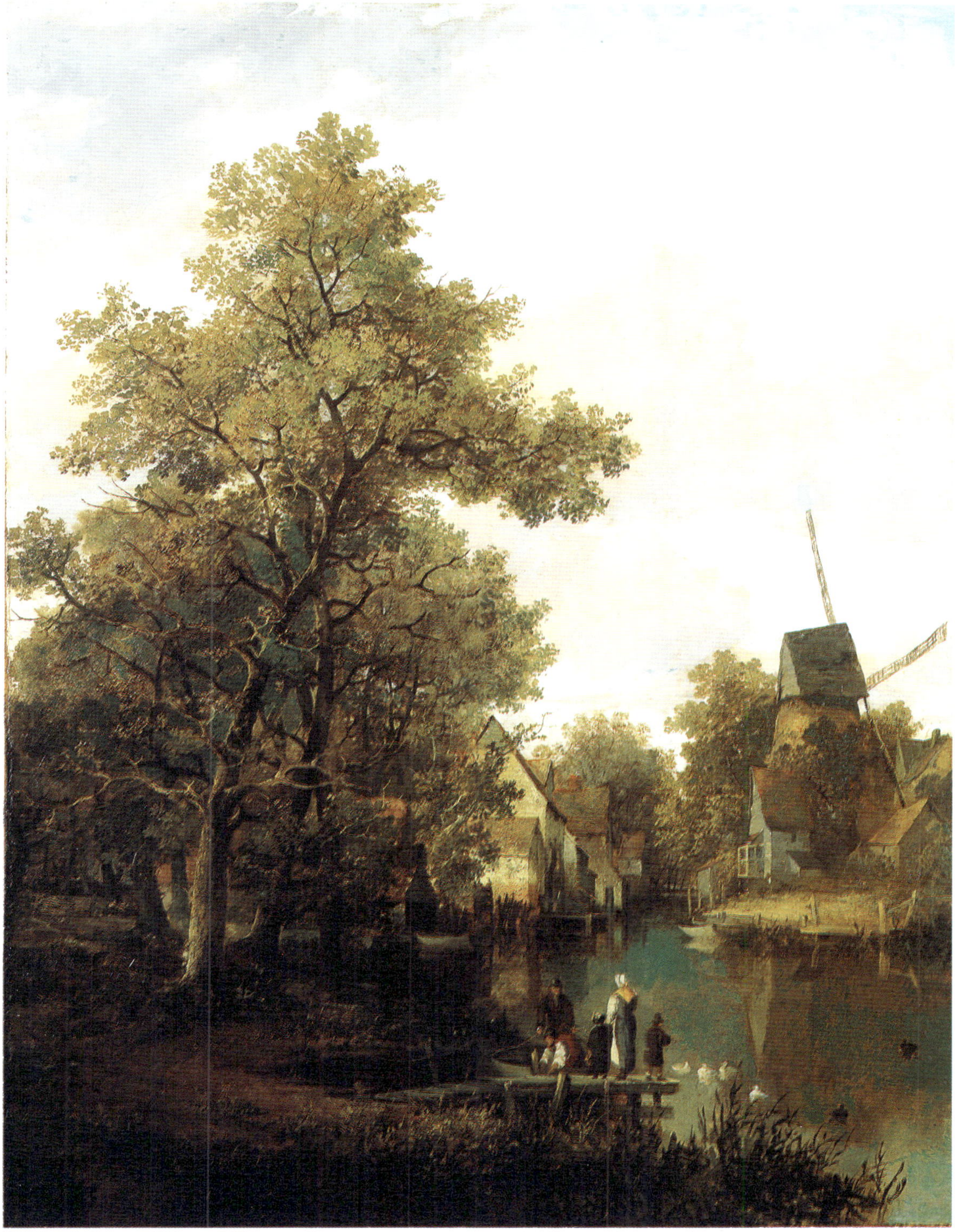

James Glen Wilson
(Irish, 1827-63)

24. Emigrant Ship Leaving Belfast (1852)

Inscr: 'J. Glen Wilson 1852' b.l.
Oil on canvas 71.4 x 91.3 cm.
Purchased 1953.

Landscape and marine painter James Glen Wilson, who came from County Down, was supposedly self-taught, although he may have attended private classes in Belfast during the early 1850s. He served as a ship's artist with the Royal Navy 1852-9 and thereafter worked as a surveyor in Australia, where he died in 1863. This painting shows a departing ship being towed out of Belfast harbour, probably en route to America. The overall feeling in the image is one of sadness and loss.

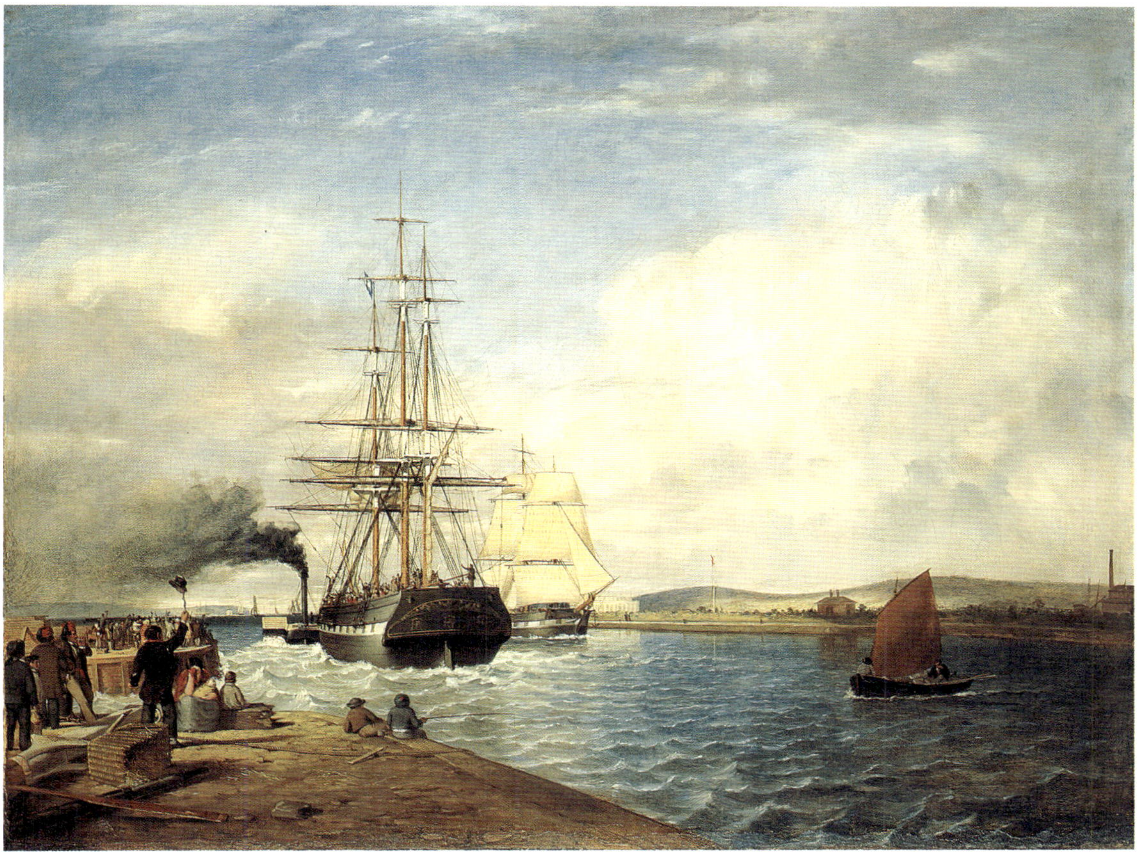

Bartholomew Colles Watkins
(Irish, 1833-91)

25. Ecclesiastical Ruins Of Inniscaltra, Or Holy Island, Lough Derg, County Galway, After Sunset: "This Island Is One Of Great Historic Interest ..." - Petrie
(c.1863)

Inscr: 'B. Colles Watkins RHA' b.r.
Oil on canvas 104.3 x 153 cm.
Purchased 1968.

Watkins began exhibiting landscapes at the Royal Hibernian Academy in 1856 and was one of its most active members, being secretary for a number of years. He specialized in Irish mountain scenery, such as in the Killarney area and in monastic ruins and castles in various parts of the country. Inniscaltra is in the area of Lough Derg situated in County Clare and not in County Galway, as stated in the title. The painting, with its emphasis on Ireland's Celtic past, shows the influence of the Celtic Revival.

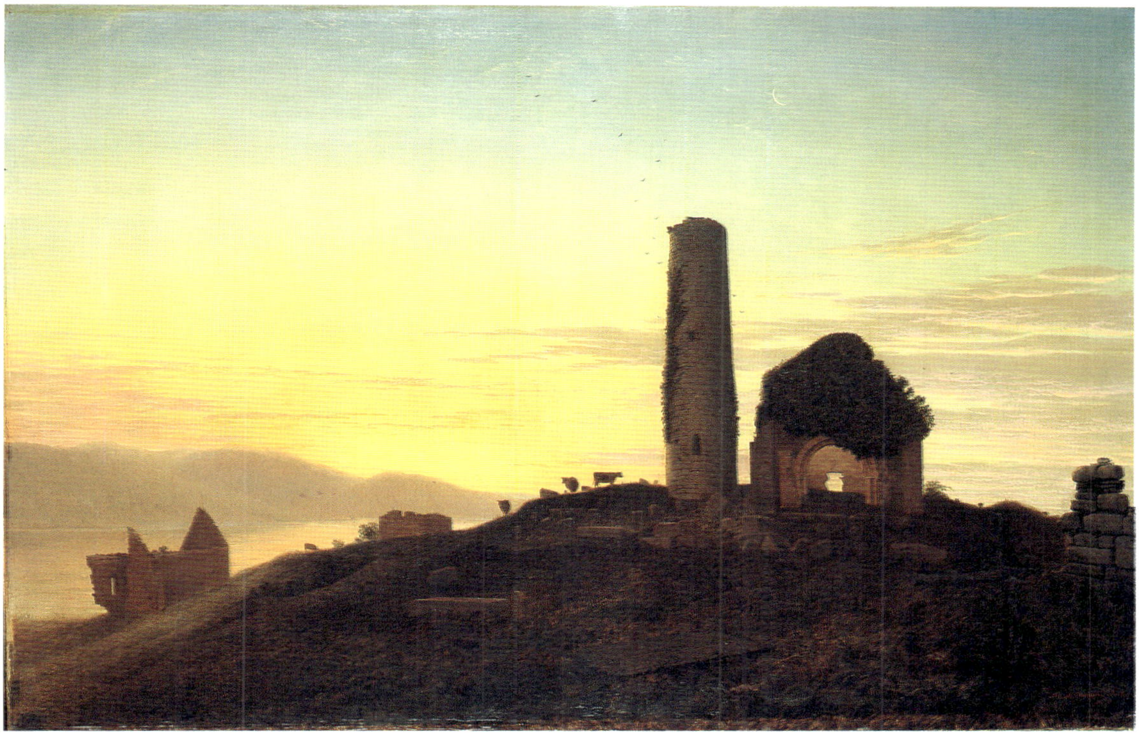

Henry Marriot Paget
(British, 1856-1936)

26. William Butler Yeats (1865-1939) (1889)

Inscr: 'W. B. Yeats by H. M. Paget April 6th 1889' b.l.
Oil on canvas 52.1 x 42.1 cm.
Donated by the Friends of the National Collections of Ireland, 1932.

Paget, a painter of portraits, historical subjects and illustrator, studied at the Royal Academy schools and exhibited at the Academy 1879-94. He became friendly with the Yeats family when they lived in Bedford Park, London 1888-1902 and often invited John Butler Yeats, father of the sitter, to share his studio, for the pleasure of his company and conversation. This portrait of William Butler Yeats, one of the most illustrious poets of this century, was painted in Bedford Park. It was there that Yeats met and fell hopelessly in love with the Irish revolutionary Maud Gonne, who became the inspiration of some of his finest work.

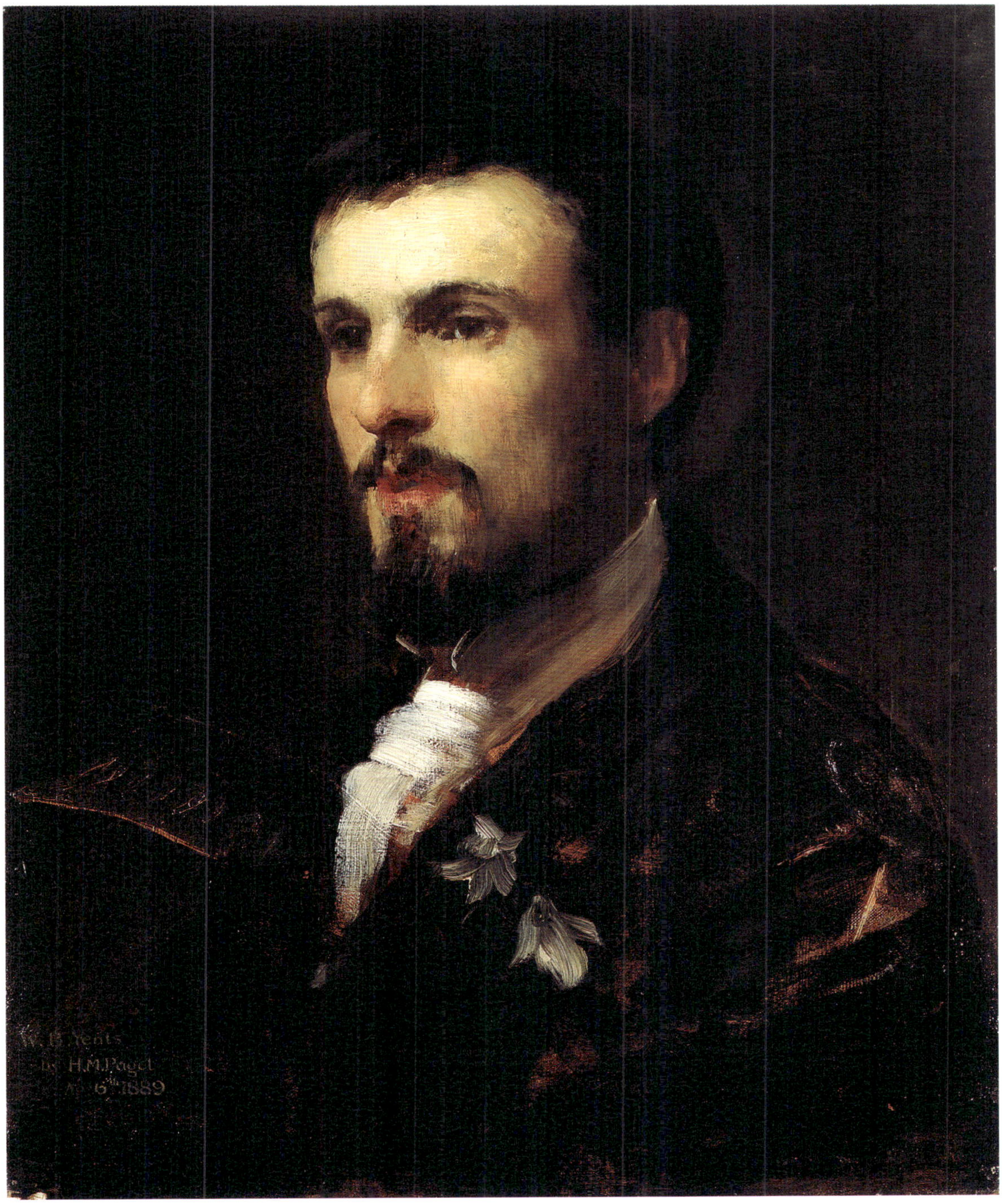
Yeats
by H.M.Paget
6th 1889

John Clayton Adams
(British, 1840-1906)

27. The Cherry Orchard

Inscr: 'J. Clayton Adams' b.r.
Oil on canvas 61.5 x 91.9 cm.
Purchased 1890.

The English landscape painter John Clayton Adams painted scenes mainly in Surrey and in the southern counties of England. An exhibitor at the Royal Academy and at other leading London art societies, his landscapes are nostalgic depictions of rural life in the late Victorian era. *The Cherry Orchard*, painted in the rich broad technique typical of his style, is a striking image of the fruitfulness and fecundity of springtime.

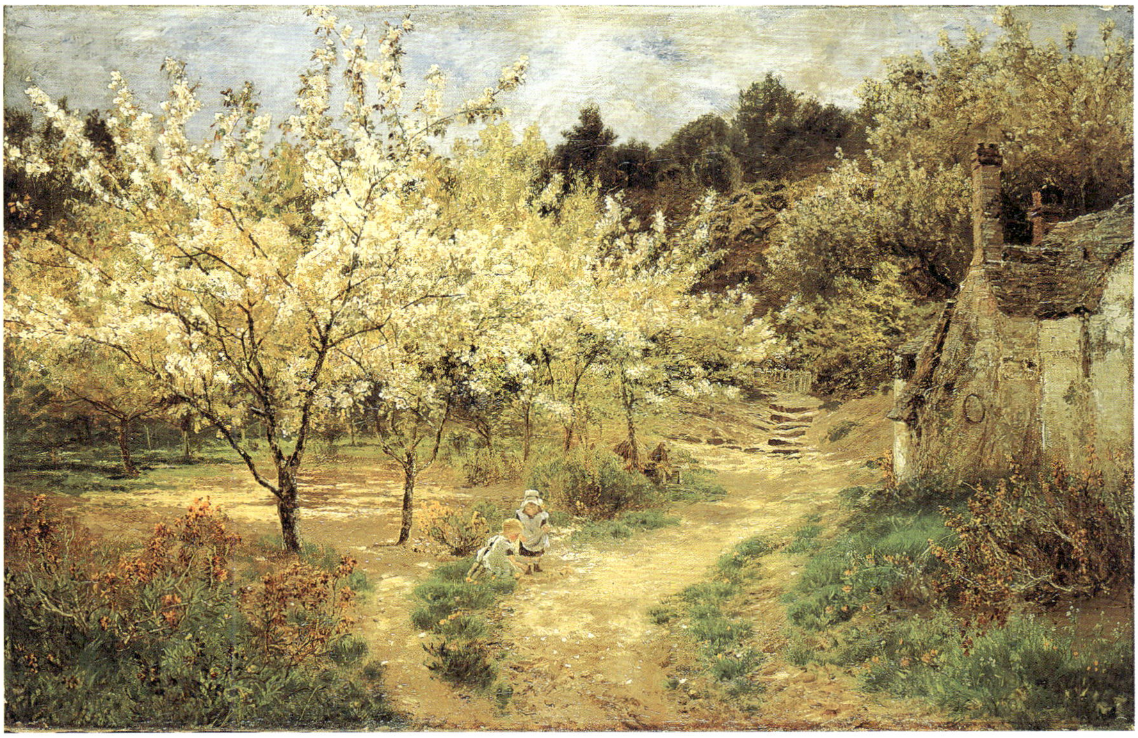

Edmund Morison Wimperis
(British, 1835-1900)

28. Landscape With Windmill
(1888)

Inscr: 'EMW 88' b.r.

Oil on canvas 127.5 x 77 cm.

Donated by Lady Cleaver, Belfast, 1936, in memory of her husband, Sir James Frederick Cleaver.

Wimperis commenced his career by studying wood engraving and worked as an illustrator for *The Illustrated London News* and other magazines but eventually took up landscape painting in oil and watercolour. He was elected a member of the Royal Institute of Painters in Watercolours in 1875 and its president twenty years later. He favoured windswept moorland scenes such as this above picturesque pastoral landscapes of hedgerows and fields.

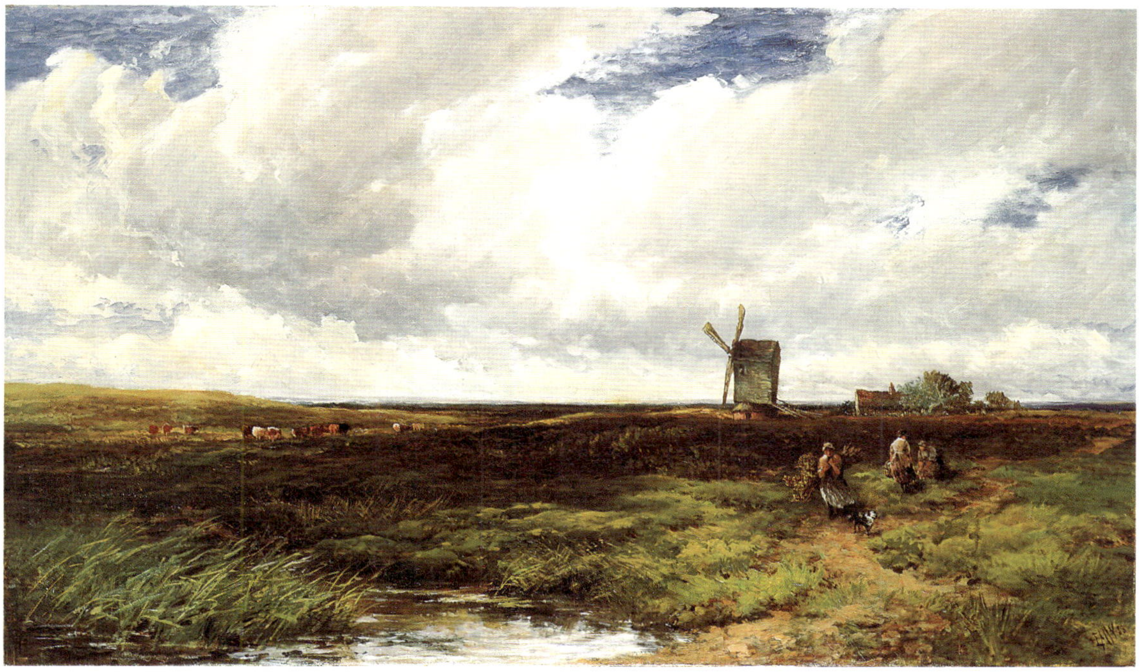

Frank O'Meara
(Irish, 1853-88)

29. Autumnal Sorrows
(1878)

Inscr: 'Frank O'Meara' b.l.
Oil on canvas 48.5 x 99.8 cm.
Purchased 1980.

One of the foremost Irish exponents of *plein air* painting in the later nineteenth century, O'Meara studied in Paris in the early 1870s and in 1875, settled in Grez-sur-Loing, a picturesque village in the forest of Fontainebleu, favoured by English, Scottish and American painters. *Autumnal Sorrows*, which shows the well-known and often-painted bridge of Grez, is his earliest extant painting. His work, poetic in subject matter and often haunting and sad in mood, has recently undergone a reassessment, after being virtually forgotten for many years.

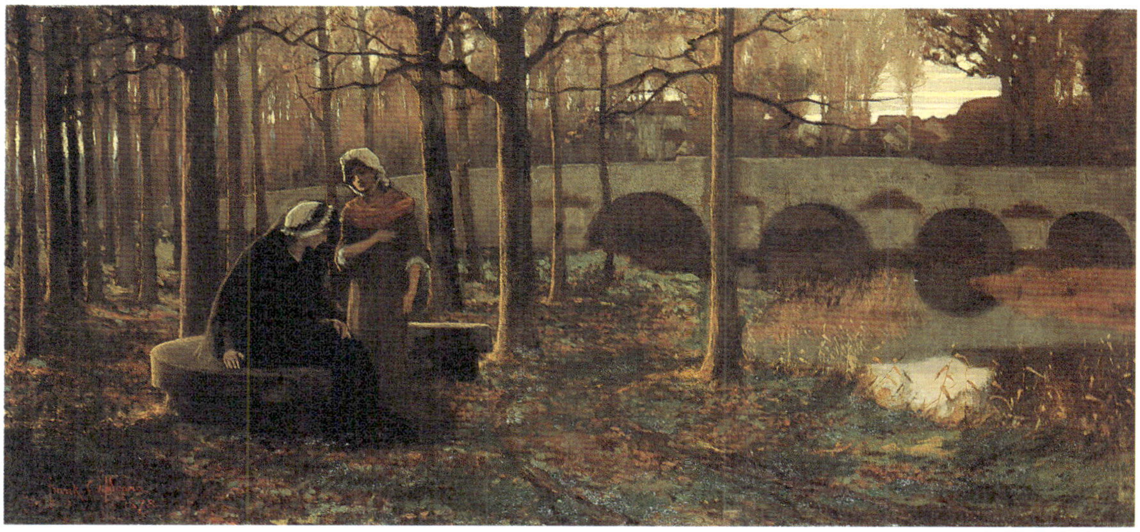

Walter Osborne
(Irish, 1859-1903)

30. Cherry Ripe
(1889)

Inscr: 'Walter Osborne 89' b.r. (date indistinct).
Oil on canvas 68.5 x 50.5 cm.
Purchased 1951.

Osborne was one of the most important Irish landscape, portrait and genre painters of the second half of the nineteenth century. He studied in Dublin and Antwerp and spent some time in France where he came under the influence of *plein air* painting. He subsequently made Dublin his base from about 1884 and worked increasingly around the city and adjacent villages from the late 1880s. This painting of a street scene is an evocative depiction of urban life at the end of the last century.

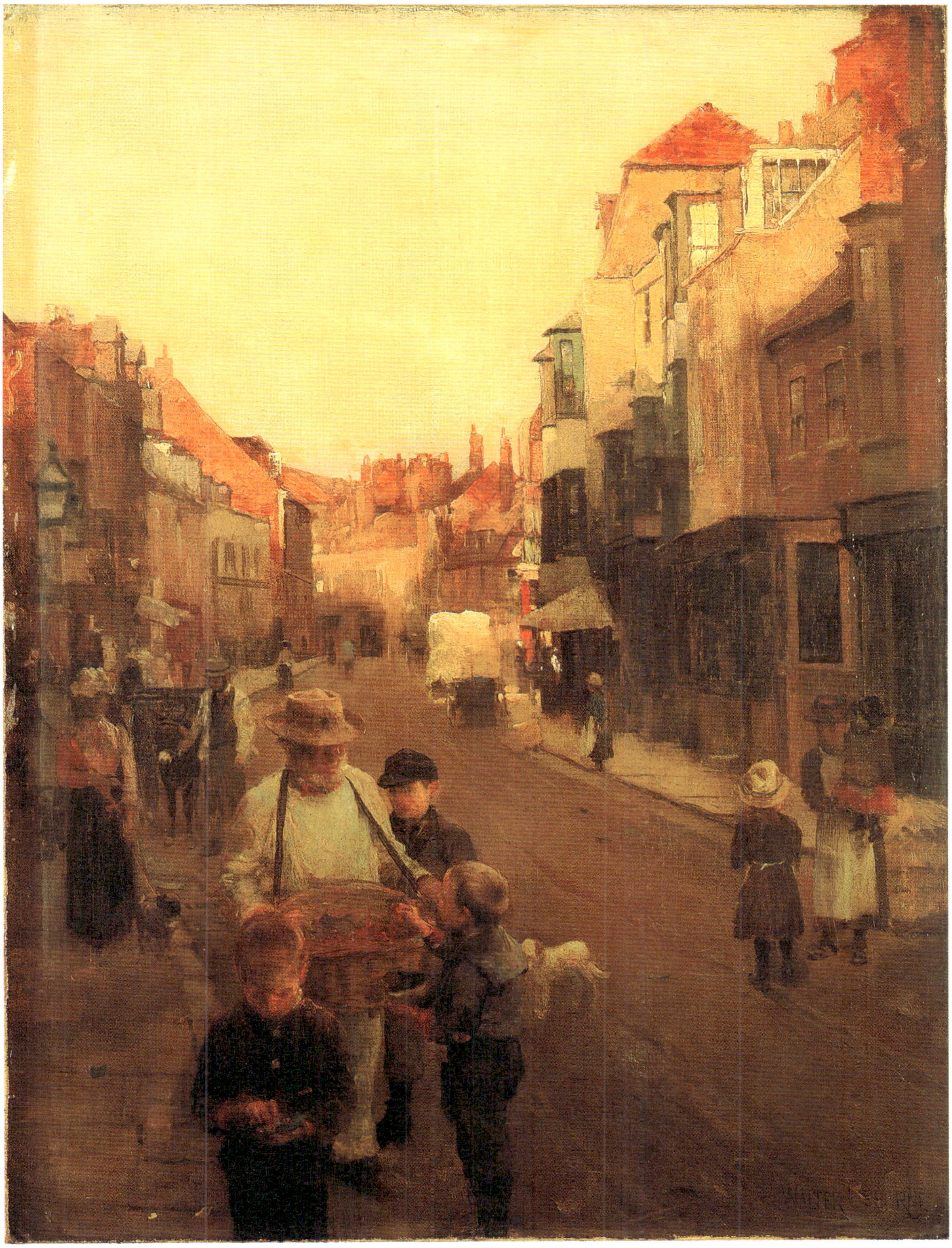

Roderic O'Conor
(Irish, 1860-1940)

31. View Of Pont Aven
(1899)

Inscr: 'R. O'Conor '99' b.r.

Oil on canvas 54.5 x 65 cm.

Purchased 1983.

At some time in 1899 O'Conor returned to Pont-Aven, where he had earlier painted in company with Gauguin. This painting, one of a number painted at this time, shows a development of his style. Over a lightly stained ground he has quickly applied brush marks and jabs of colour in contrast with areas where the paint seems to have come directly from the tube and been mixed on the canvas. A new colour range, bringing in blues, pinks and mauve appears in his paintings of the buildings. The earlier Pont-Aven striping has gone, being scarcely referred to at all except in the distant hills where a very mild version is hinted at. The overall impression is of speed, vigour and energy in the execution of this landscape, which appears to have been painted wholly from observation.

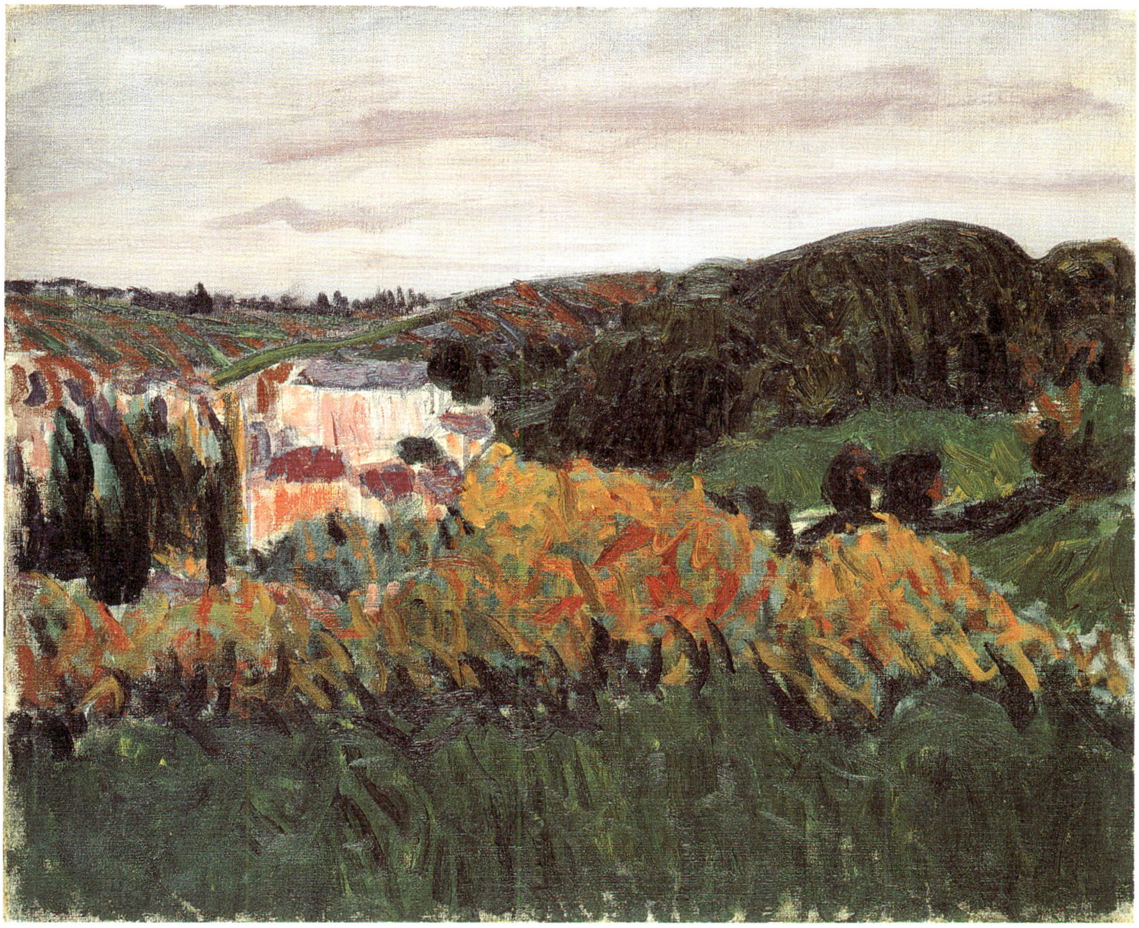

Frank McKelvey
(Irish, 1895-1974)

32. EVENING, BALLYCASTLE
(c.1924)

Inscr: 'Frank McKelvey' b.l.
Oil on canvas 76.5 x 102 cm.
Purchased 1924

Frank McKelvey was one of the most popular landscapists working in Ireland in the inter-war years and immediately after. As can be seen here, his style was highly accomplished and always he conveyed a feeling of airy spaciousness. He worked a good deal in Counties Antrim and Donegal. As with F. W. Hull, the lightness of his touch provided a contrast to the more moody landscapes of Paul Henry, Charles Lamb, James Humbert Craig and many others who worked in the west.

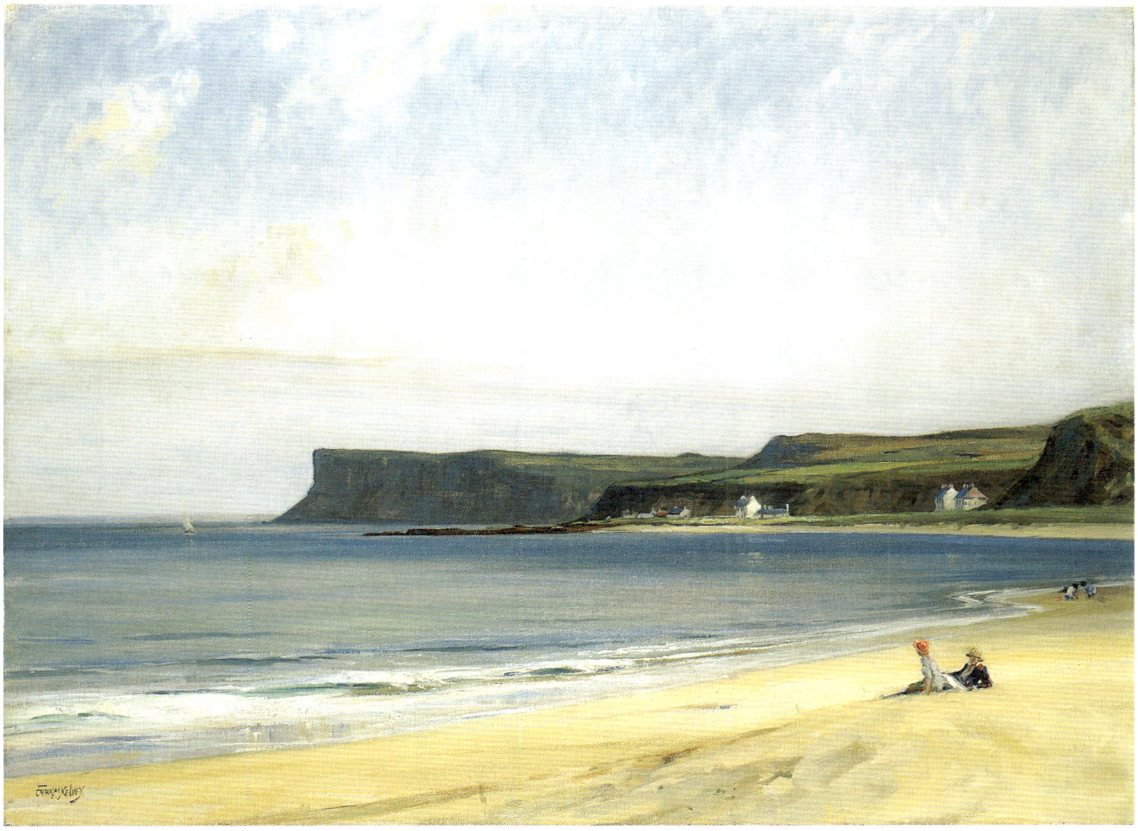

Georgina Moutray Kyle
(Irish, 1865-1950)

33. The Lifting Of The Fog At The Gasworks, Belfast
(c.1926)

Inscr: 'G. Moutray Kyle' b.l.

Oil on canvas 55.1 x 73.5 cm.

Bequeathed by the artist, 1950.

Georgina Moutray Kyle was one of the foremost women artists in Belfast in the first half of the twentieth century. Her work, which encompassed market scenes and harbour views, flowers and still life, is highly distinctive and easily recognised because of its linear emphasis and strong use of pattern. This painting, which was executed from a spot on the Ormeau Embankment, is a striking image of a relatively mundane urban scene.

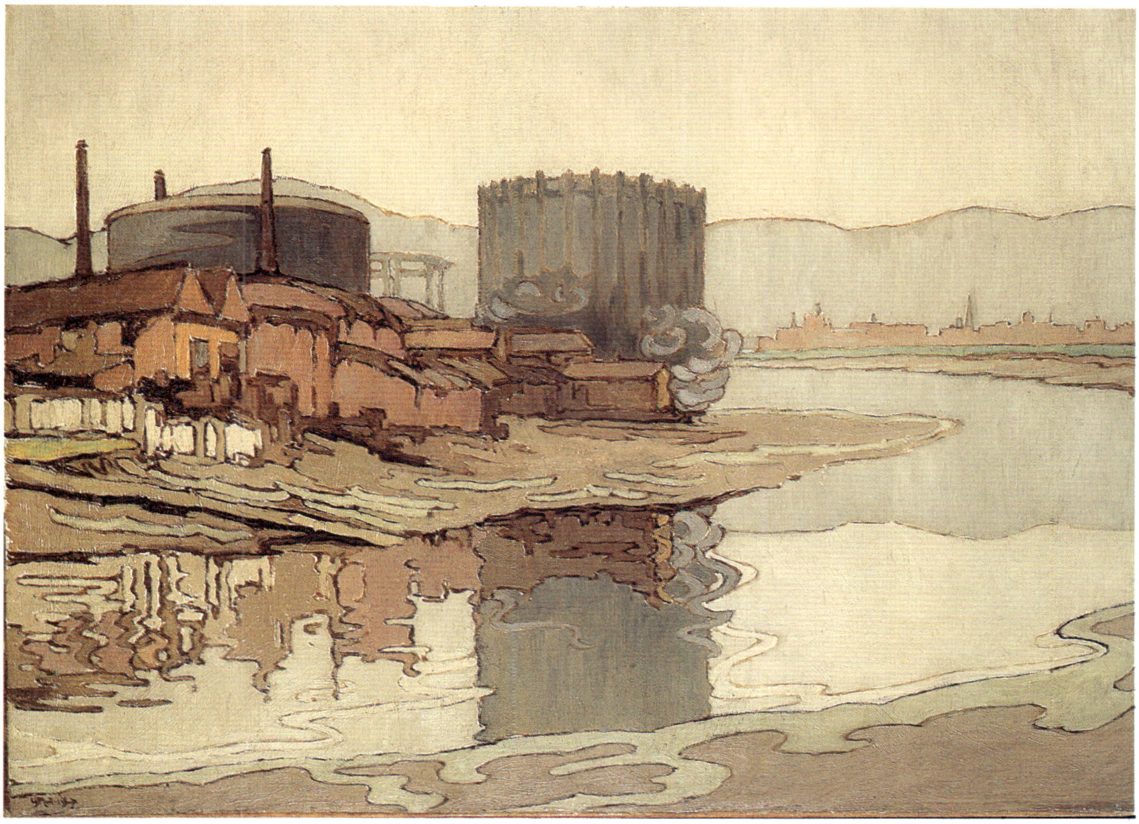

Ben Nicholson
(British, 1894-1982)

34. Painting, 1935
(1935)

Inscr: 'Ben Nicholson 1935' on stretcher.
Oil on canvas 71.1 x 92.1 cm.
Purchased 1967.

Ben Nicholson was one of the first English artists of his generation to embrace abstract painting in the mid-1930s. In much of his subsequent work, as here, he juxtaposed geometrical shapes, often in relief, so as to explore effects of balance, shape and texture in a rather Platonic manner.

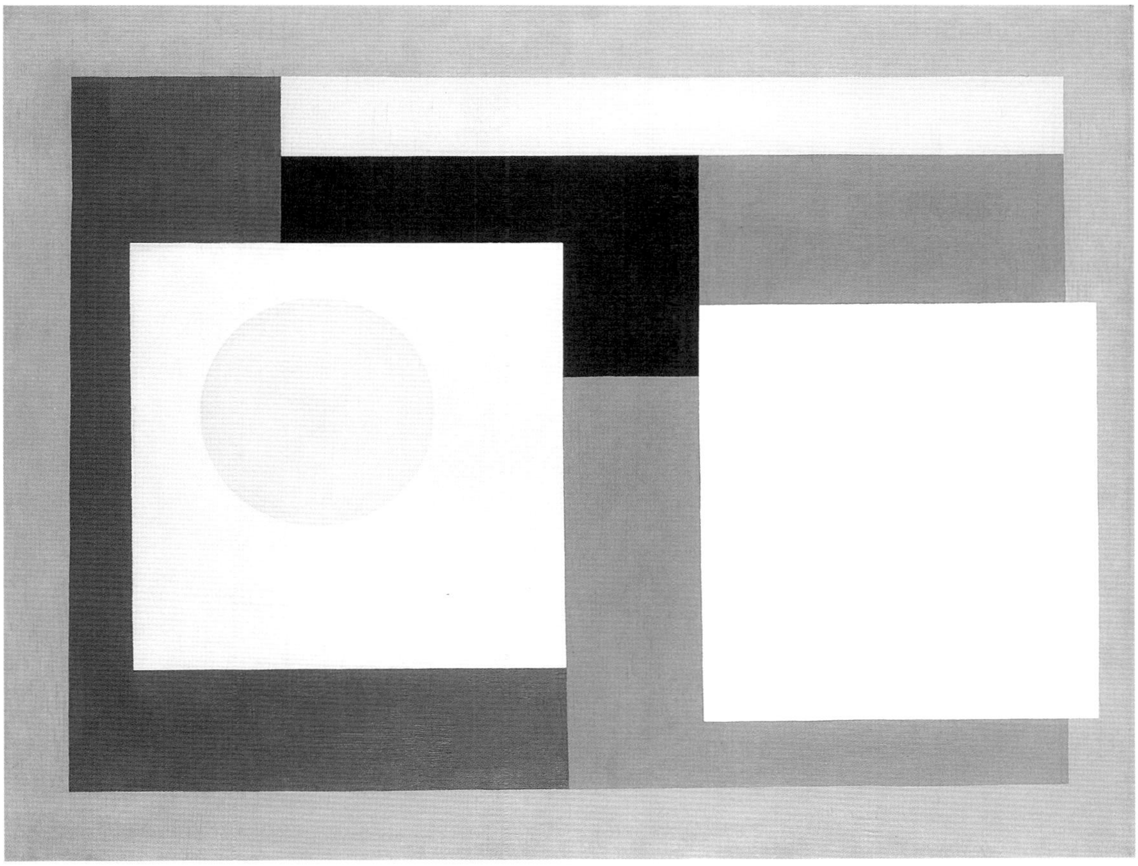

Graham Sutherland
(British, 1903-80)

35. Gorse On A Sea Wall
(1939)

Inscr: 'Graham Sutherland 1939' b.l.

Oil on canvas 62.2 x 48.3 cm.

Purchased 1967.

Much of Graham Sutherland's work evolved from an examination of organic growth and other natural structures. Here, in one of his most important pictures from the immediate pre-war period, he is not concerned to describe the appearance of the landscape, or of a piece of gorse in particular, but rather to convey the natural attributes - its pricklieness, for example - of the gorse.

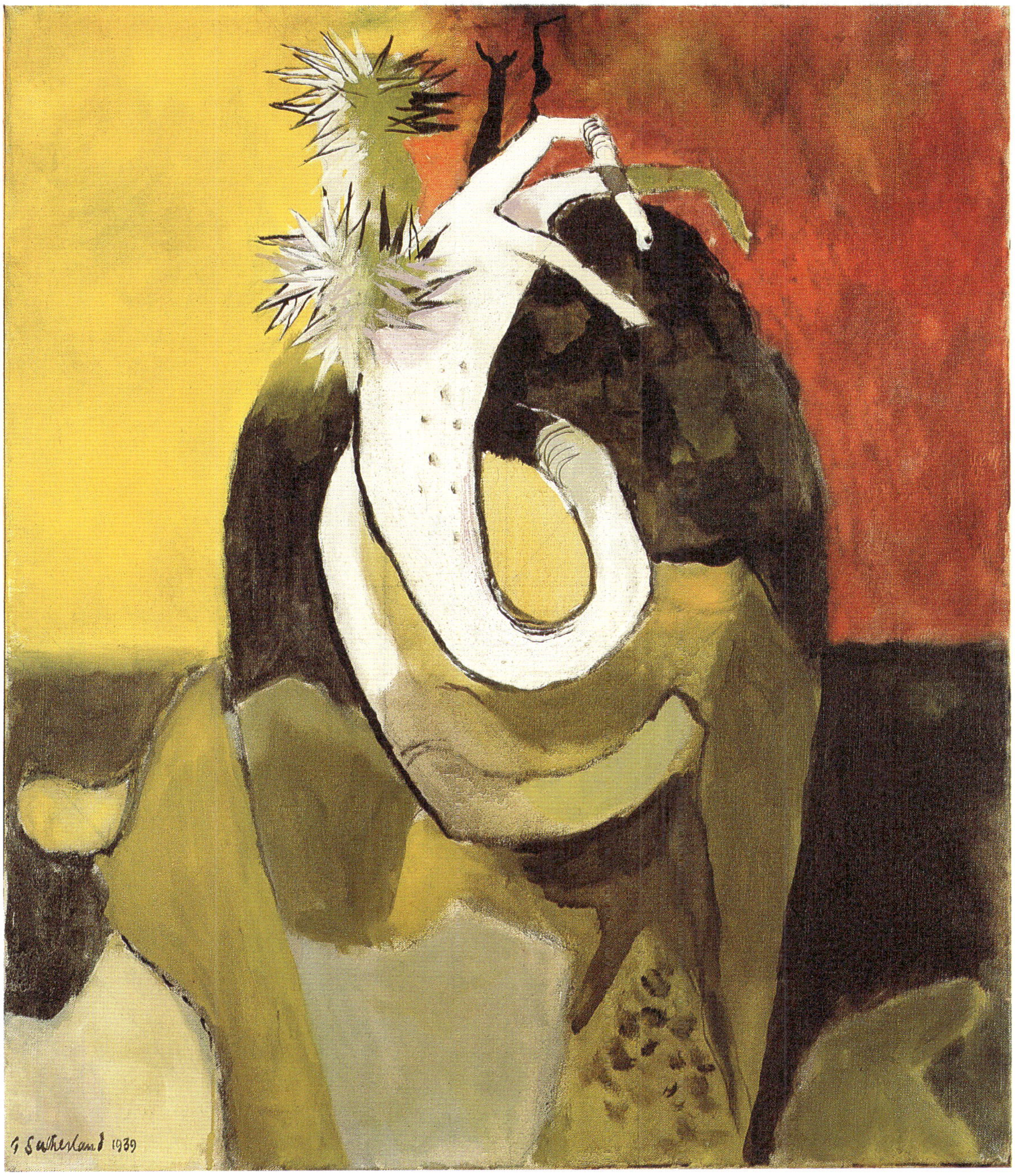
G Sutherland 1939

Leo Whelan
(Irish, 1892-1956)

36. Interior Of A Kitchen
(c.1934)

Inscr: 'Leo Whelan' b.r.
Oil on canvas 68.3 x 57.5 cm.
Donated by the Thomas Haverty Trust,
Dublin, 1941.

Leo Whelan, as can be seen from this composition, was a superb painter of genre scenes. He was much influenced by the seventeenth century Dutch painter Jan Vermeer and was adept at rendering the inherent nature, texture and surface quality of different materials, such as the glass bowl, the wicker-work basket, the fruit and the wooden table top on which they are laid out in this scene, which was painted in the kitchen of his own house in Dublin.

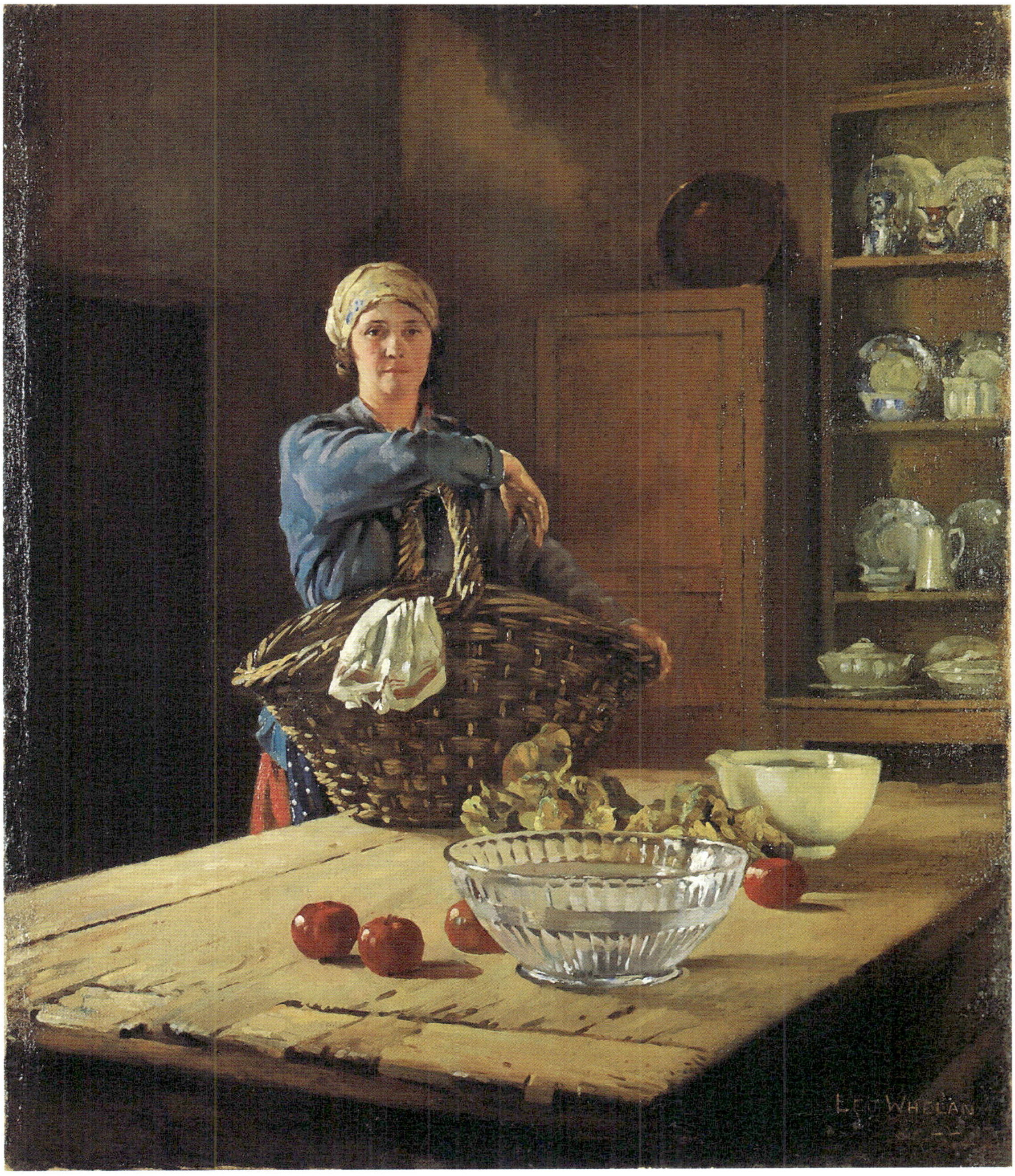
LEO WHELAN

John Luke
(Irish, 1906-75)

37. The Three Dancers
(1945)

Inscr: 'Luke' b.r.
Oil and tempera on canvas on board 30.7 x 43 cm.
Purchased 1945.

This composition illustrates the highly stylized manner for which John Luke is famed. Executed in tempera on canvas, the technique exemplifies his emphasis on drawing, an approach which he adopted during his years as a student at the Slade School of Art in London.

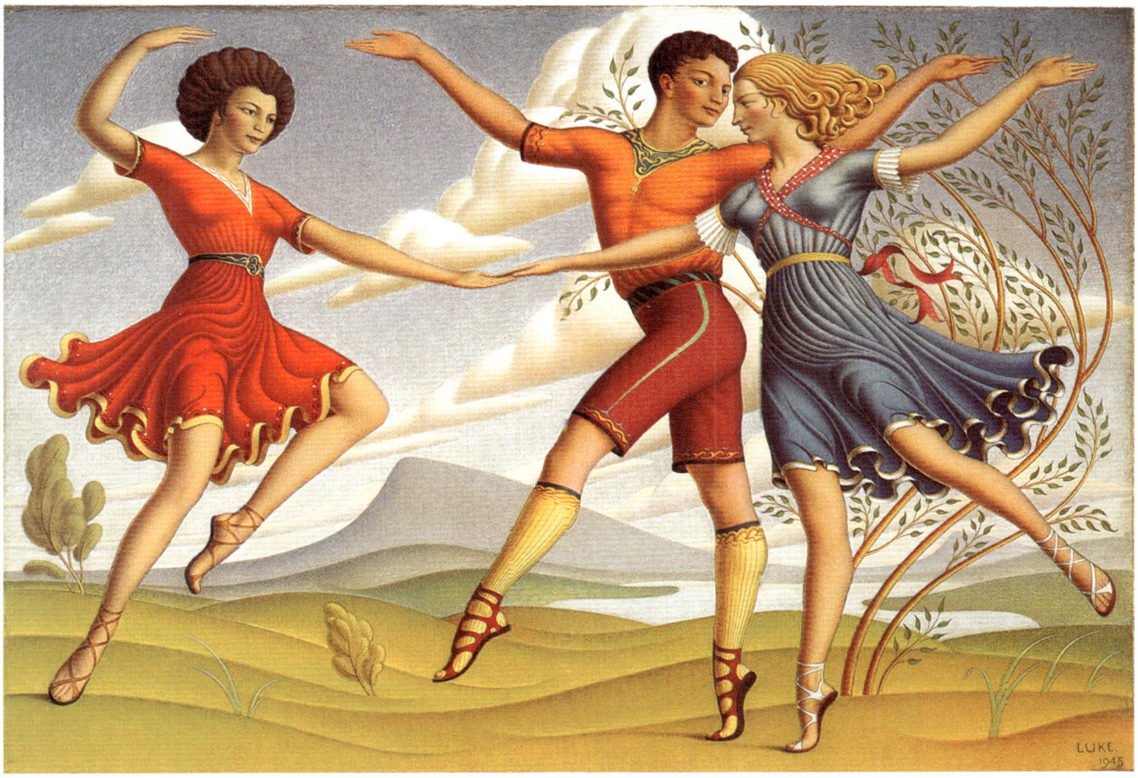
LUKE
1945

Gerard Dillon
(Irish, 1916-71)

38. Yellow Bungalow
(1954)

Inscr: 'Gerard Dillon' b.r.
Oil on canvas 76.8 x 81.2 cm.
Donated by the Thomas Haverty Trust,
Dublin, 1956.

Dillon was one of the most influential Irish painters of his generation. Much of his subject-matter was based on scenes of everyday life and he often depicted his friends at work and at play. Yet, as here, one feels that the real thrust of Dillon's painting is something deeper, more philosophical; what one might call the 'human condition'.

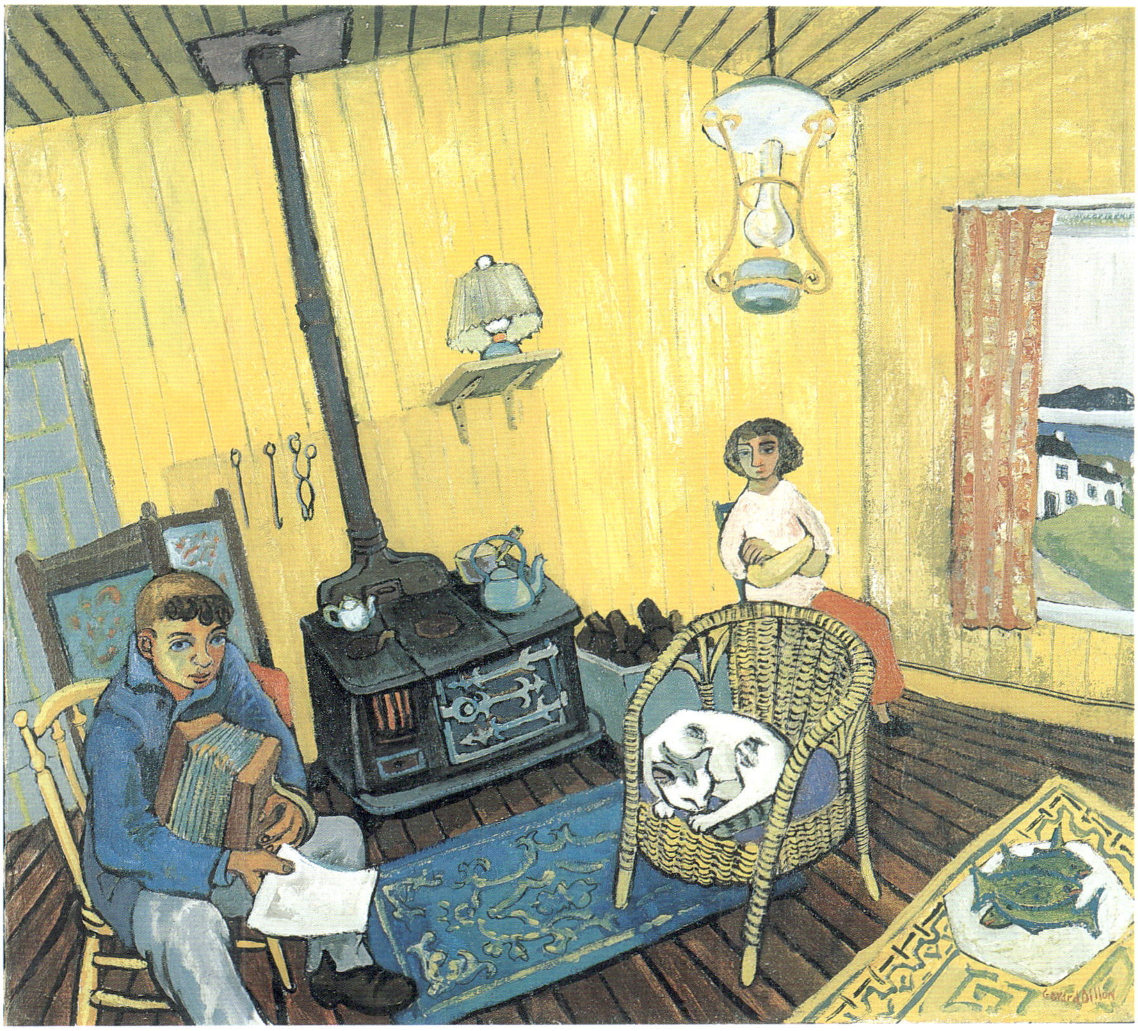

William Scott
(Irish, worked in Britain, 1913-89)

39. White With Red Lines
(1962)

Inscr: 'W. Scott' b.r.
Oil on canvas 86 x 111.5 cm.
Purchased 1983.

This composition, with the various elements simplified to near - symbols of their kind, is typical of Scott's early still life work. The emphasis on the purity of simple forms directly stated is, too, characteristic of the kind of work, often abstract, practised by those painters who lived in Cornwall.

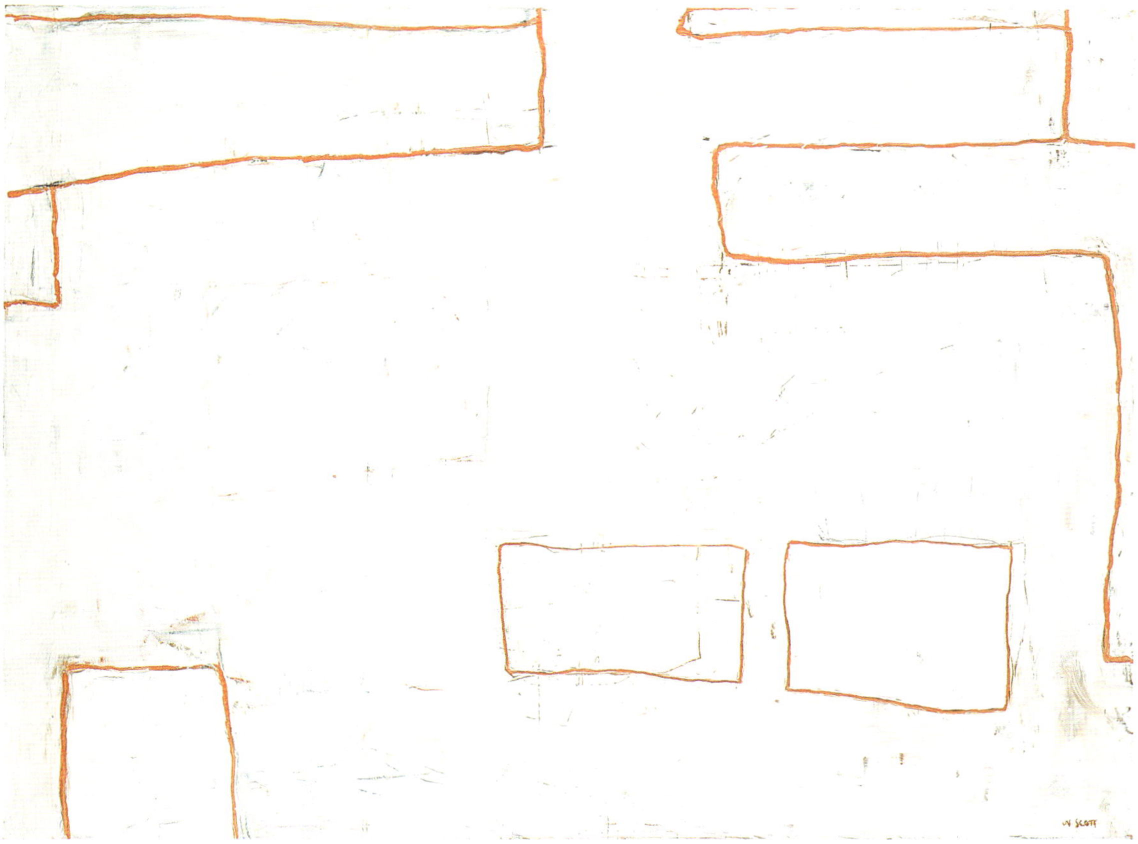
W SCOTT

Roger Hilton
(British, 1911-75)

40. January 1962
(1962)

Inscr: 'Hilton Jan '62 45 x 50' on back of canvas.
Oil on canvas 113.8 x 126.9 cm.
Purchased 1962.

Although Roger Hilton's work is almost entirely abstract his imagery is often derived from landscape and to a large extent embodies his feelings for place, mood and atmosphere. He once wrote that in titling his pictures he wrote down 'the first thing that came into his head', but, nevertheless, his work is largely autobiographical.

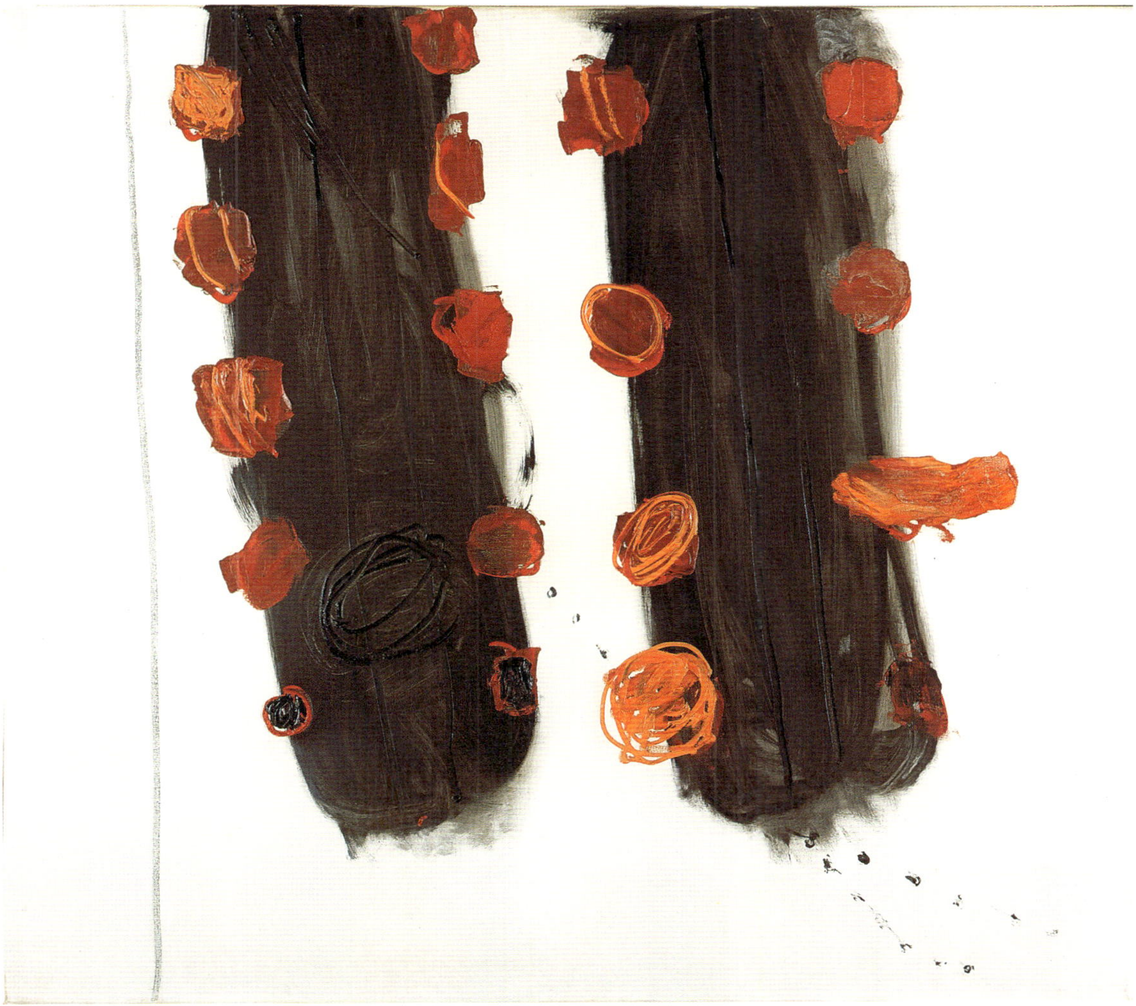

Sidney Ivon Hitchens
(British, 1893-1979)

41. Spring In Autumn
(1967)

Inscr: 'Hitchens 67' b.r.

Oil on canvas 58.8 x 155.2 cm.

Purchased 1969.

Ivon Hitchens, an Englishman, is best remembered as a painter of landscapes, flowers and still lifes. While his work verged on the abstract it never became completely so. Colour, used with an almost gay abandon, is a characteristic of his work and that is seen to good effect here.

T. P. Flanagan
(Irish, b. 1929)

42. GORTAHORK (2)
(1967)

Inscr: 'T. P. Flanagan' b.r.
Oil and acrylic on board 92.2 x 118.9 cm.
Purchased 1969.

This picture was painted during the artist's first visit with his friend the poet Seamus Heaney, to Gortahork, County Donegal, a village on the extreme north coast of Ireland. It belongs to a set of pictures collectively entitled *Boglands*, which inspired the poem of the same title which Heaney dedicated to Flanagan at this time. The picture is an amalgam of views made from drawings done in the locality of Gortahork.

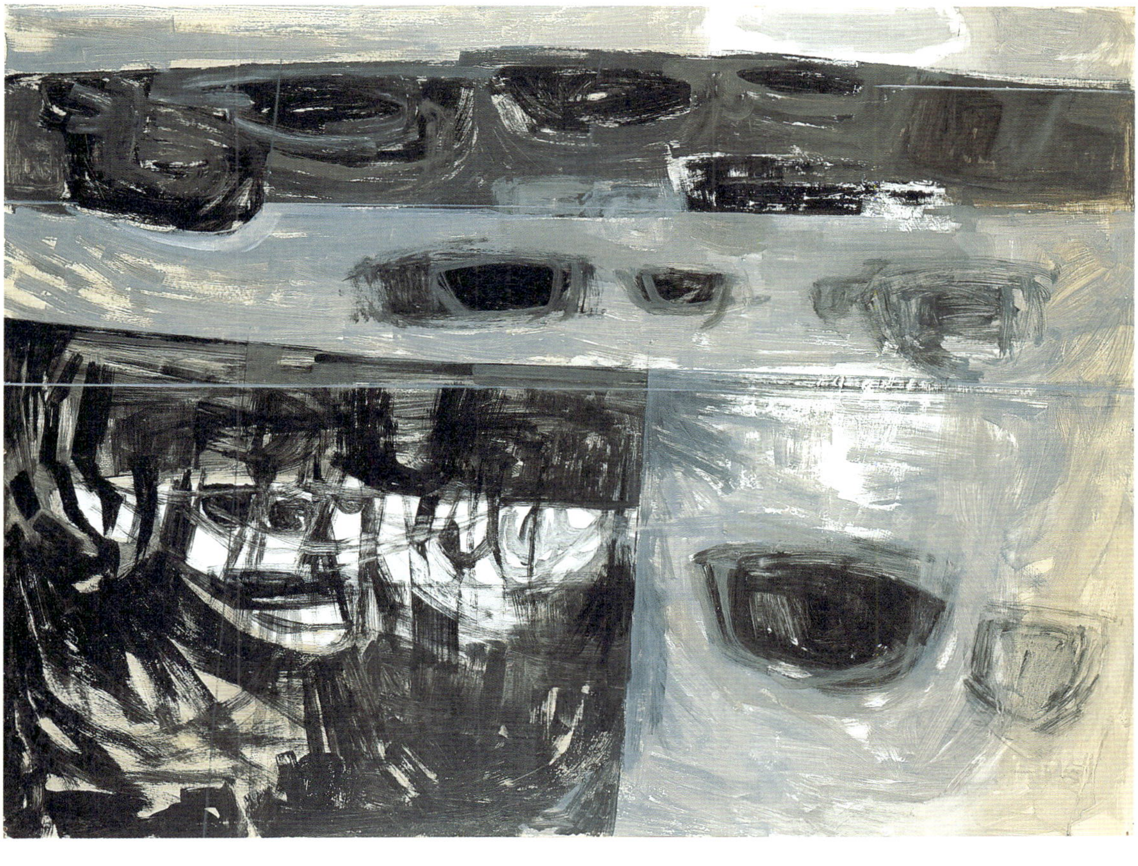

Stephen McKenna
(British, b.1939)

43. Maritime Still Life
(1988)

Inscr: 'S. McK' b.r.

Oil on canvas 120 x 160 cm.

Purchased 1989.

Stephen McKenna was born in England of Irish descent. He spends part of each year in County Donegal where this picture was painted. As here, his subject-matter generally has a mildly Surrealist edge with familiar objects being placed in slightly unnatural settings. McKenna was nominated for the Turner Prize in 1987.

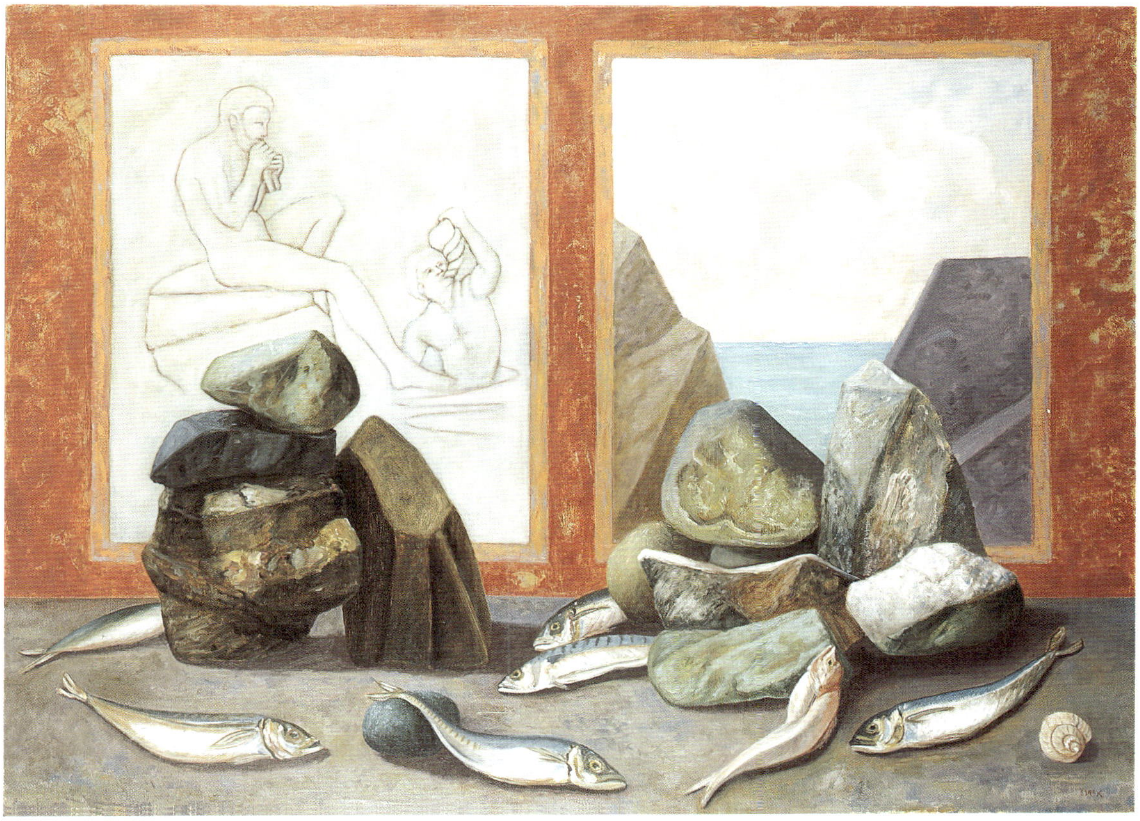

Joseph McWilliams
(Irish, b. 1938)

44. The Governors Of Anguilla, Gibraltar, The Caymen Islands And The Last Governor Of Northern Ireland (1989)

Inscr: 'Joseph McWilliams 1989' b.r.
Oil on canvas 152.3 x 213.4 cm.
Purchased 1989.

As this picture illustrates, Joseph McWilliams is a fine colourist and, also as here, he embodies in his work a compelling sense of movement, of things in flux. Much of his work is topical in subject-matter, being related to current events and to the 'Troubles' of Northern Ireland.

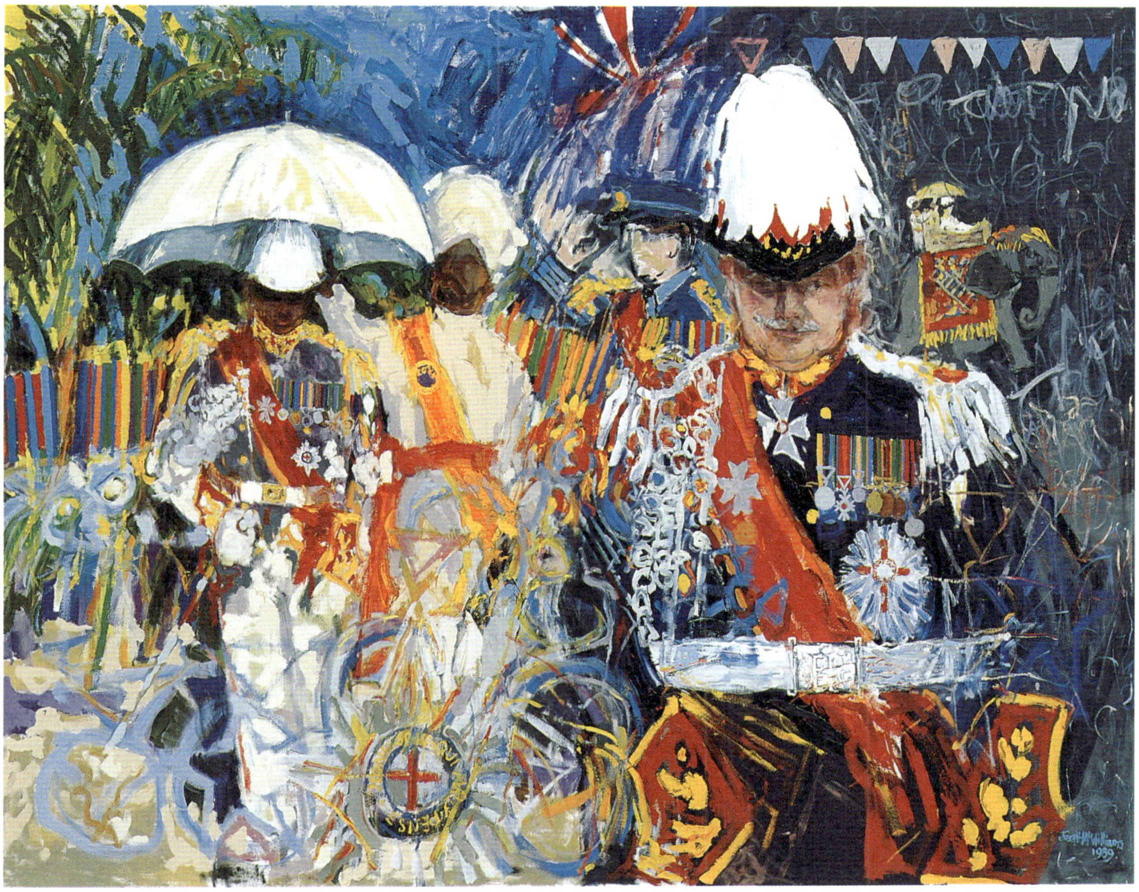

Basil Blackshaw
(Irish, b. 1932)

45. The Barn (BLUE II)
(1993)

Inscr: 'Blackshaw' t.r.

Oil on canvas 50.8 x 61 cm.

Purchased 1992.

Basil Blackshaw is one of the most important Ulster painters of his generation. Much of his work is concerned with people and animals and attitudes towards life. He has always worked in a free, *malerisch* manner, placing emphasis on the act of painting and making play with his materials, so that obtrusive brushwork and strong colours, such as can be seen here, are characteristic features of his paintings.

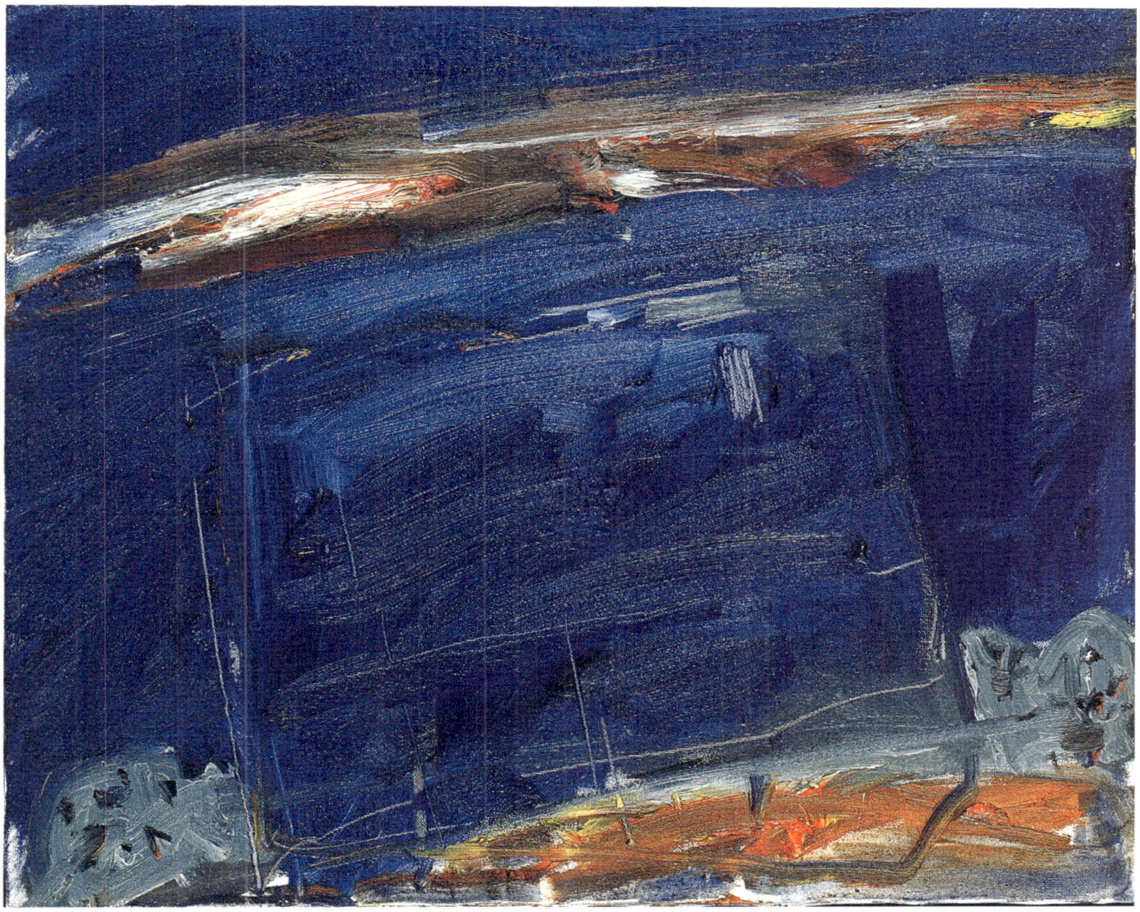

Copyright Credits

The publishers wish to thank the following for permission to reproduce work in copyright:

Basil Blackshaw for *The Barn (Blue II)* by Basil Blackshaw; © Design and Artists Copyright Society (DACS), 1997, for *Gorse on a Sea Wall* by Graham Sutherland; Gerard Dillon for *Yellow Bungalow* by Gerard Dillon; Sister Theophane Dwyer for *View of Pont Aven* by Roderic O'Conor; Terence Flanagan for *Gortahork (2)* by Terence Flanagan; © Estate of Roger Hilton, 1997, all rights reserved DACS for *January 1962* by Roger Hilton; John Hitchens for *Spring in Autumn* by Sidney Ivon Hitchens; Mrs. Sadie McKee for *The Three Dancers* by John Luke; Robert McKelvey for *Evening, Ballycastle* by Frank McKelvey; Stephen McKenna for *Maritime Still Life* by Stephen McKenna; Joseph McWilliams for *The Governors of Anguilla, Gibraltar, the Caymen Islands and the Last Governor of Northern Ireland* by Joseph McWilliams; Robert Scott for *White with Red Lines* by William Scott; © Angela Verren-Taunt, 1997, all rights reserved DACS for *Painting 1935* by Ben Nicholson.